AUG 2 1 2012

SAN DIEGO'S
JUDGE MAYOR

LIMITED EDITION

OCTOBER, 2011

NUMBER 719 OF 1000

SAN DIEGO'S JUDGE MAYOR

How Murphy's Law Blindsided
Leadership with 2020 Vision

Judge Dick Murphy

33RD MAYOR OF SAN DIEGO

Sunbelt Publications
San Diego, California

San Diego's Judge Mayor
Sunbelt Publications, Inc.
Copyright © 2011 by Richard Murphy
All rights reserved.
First edition, 2011

ISBN: 978-0-9620402-4-5 (hardcover)
978-0-9620402-7-6 (paperback)
978-0-9620402-8-3 (ebook)

Copyediting by Laurie Gibson
Jacket and interior design and composition by Lydia D'moch
Project Management by Karla Olson, BookStudio
Printed in the United States of America

Sunbelt Publications, Inc.
P.O. Box 191126
San Diego, CA 92159-1126
(619) 258-4911, fax: (619) 258-4916
www.sunbeltbooks.com

Publisher's Cataloging in Publication Data
Murphy, Richard M., 1942–
San Diego's judge mayor : how Murphy's Law blindsided leadership with 2020 vision /
Dick Murphy.—1st ed.—San Diego, Calif. : Sunbelt Publications, c2011.
p. ; cm.
ISBN: 978-0-9620402-4-5 (hardcover); 978-0-9620402-7-6 (paperback);
978-0-9620402-8-3 (ebook)
Includes index.
1. Murphy, Richard M., 1941– 2. San Diego (Calif.)—Politics and government.
3. San Diego (Calif.)—Economic conditions—2000- I. Title.

F869.S22 M87 2011   2011934731
320.9/794985—dc23   1109

Unless otherwise specified, all photos are from
the personal collection of Richard and Janice Murphy.

This book is dedicated to my wife Jan,
mother of our three children Brian, Shannon, and Kelly,
whose support and encouragement for
more than four decades made this journey possible.

CONTENTS

Prologue

An Invitation
and a Warning

I HAD THE HONOR OF BEING ELECTED the 33rd mayor of San Diego—
and the first San Diego mayor of the 21st century. It was a good time to
take the helm at the city. At the start of a new millennium, the mood was
ebullient, and I believed that this public hopefulness would help support
the development of important civic projects.

In December 2000 I delivered an inaugural address as mayor entitled
"New Partnerships, New Beginnings." One month later I gave my first
State of the City address, titled "A Vision for San Diego in the Year 2020,"
outlining 10 goals for the city. Brimming with optimism, I promised to
deliver "leadership with 2020 vision."

Four and a half years later, I announced my resignation because I
thought it would be best for the city. Much had been accomplished, but
we had been battered by a pension deficit and other unforeseen problems.
The earlier optimism was gone and the political mood had soured to the
point of no return.

This book is about that journey—how events earlier in my life led me to run for mayor, how we pulled off a surprise upset victory in the San Diego mayoral election of 2000, how we went about implementing my vision for San Diego in the year 2020, and how my leadership with 2020 vision was eventually blindsided by Murphy's Law: Anything that can go wrong will go wrong.

The book has several purposes. It offers to readers an insider's perspective of the mayoral election of 2000 and my time as mayor. It also discusses lessons I learned as mayor as well as earlier in my life as a high school and college student, an Army officer, San Diego City councilmember, and Superior Court judge. Finally, I share some thoughts about the future of our great city and some ideas that I believe would make it even greater.

Woven throughout the book are three themes. First, you have to take some risks in life if you intend to make a difference. Second, for those who are attentive, God will open doors and invite you to cross the threshold. Third, hard work and persistence are more important than natural talent in achieving success.

This book is both an invitation and a warning. The invitation is to seek to be all you can be and try to make a difference. The warning is that the best intentions can be misunderstood and sidetracked by events beyond your control.

Regardless, I would commend to my readers to follow the admonition of Irish author George Bernard Shaw when he wrote:

Life is no brief candle to me. It is a sort of splendid torch which I have got a hold of for the moment, and I want to make it burn as brightly as possible before handing it onto future generations.

SAN DIEGO'S
JUDGE MAYOR

Dickie Murphy, age six (1948)

1

GROWING UP IN ILLINOIS:
The First Big Lessons

"The lessons of their early youth regulated
the conduct of their riper years."
—*William Godwin*

MY CHILDHOOD AND HIGH SCHOOL YEARS weren't exactly a prairie idyll. But compared to the formative years of many people, they were grand. My days, especially beginning at about age 10, were filled with friends, sports, studies, and what we now call good Midwestern "values." My parents were loving, if strict. And my schools, teachers, and coaches were better than average and, in some cases, extraordinary. So I have few complaints.

Born in Oak Park, Illinois, I was raised in the fast-growing suburbs west of Chicago in the 1940s and 1950s. And, indeed, it all seemed pretty good to me at the time. Yet as I look back now on those years I see that my parents were struggling young educators trying to come to grips with an era of global political upheaval and economic uncertainty. We don't often think of that post-war era as particularly fractious compared, say, to some later decades. But remember that during the period Americans, including my folks, were leaving farms for the cities. Small towns were quickly turning into big ones. Television and other media were beginning to change families and mores, and the so-called Cold War cast a pall over nearly everything.

Growing up then, I was expected to work hard, obey, and make a future contribution to society. And I think those expectations proved to be a pretty good grounding for coming to grips with the second half of the 20th century—and beyond—in America.

My father, Robert Raymond ("Bob") Murphy, had worked his way through college during the Great Depression, graduating from the University of Illinois and becoming an elementary school principal (and eventually, assistant superintendent) in Maywood, Illinois, where we lived for the first nine years after I was born (in December 1942). My dad's forefathers had emigrated from Ireland in the 1700s and eventually became farmers in southern Illinois.

My mother, Dorothy Marguerite ("Penny") Murphy, was also an Illinois graduate. She'd met my dad at the university and later became a beloved fifth-grade teacher. Her father had emigrated from England as a child and worked as a coal miner in downstate Illinois.

Early Years in Maywood

Like so many of his generation, my dad was permanently affected by growing up during the Depression. Even though he managed to get a good education and a solid job, he was always alert for the next economic cataclysm—and he really knew how to squeeze a nickel. That likely explains why we lived for nine years in a modest, one-bedroom apartment in the suburb of Maywood, about ten miles west of downtown Chicago. I slept on a hide-a-bed in the dining room and walked several blocks to Emerson Elementary School every weekday. I often dodged pugnacious dogs along the way.

Bob and Penny Murphy (1940)

While then not a terrible, crime-ridden neighborhood, the area—laced with dirt alleys and cheap stores—was old and a bit rundown. A number of the local families were European immigrants who lived in modest apartments above the street-level retail shops. Many of the nearby houses had been built in the 19th century and, in a few cases, had been abandoned. In fact, we kids sometimes broke into them, not to steal anything but just out of curiosity and for something to do.

Childhood pleasures were simple. We played in the dirt alleys, tossing tennis balls against brick walls and even doing some "dumpster diving" in local commercial trash bins, again not of necessity but just for amusement. Like most youngsters of that era, we reenacted cowboy-and-Indian battles with cap guns and, of course, imagined ourselves as American soldiers and sailors fighting for freedom against foreign aggressors.

Because Maywood was such a transient neighborhood, I didn't make a lot of lasting friends there. But although I had no brothers or sisters, our family was reasonably close. My dad, a trim six-footer and former college athlete, was clearly the disciplinarian. But he also had an eye for family fun. For instance, he hung a miniature basketball hoop in the small foyer of our apartment, and he and I would tirelessly toss a small ball at it, seeking to ring the bell when the ball tumbled through the net. And one of my first memories involves going to a Cubs game at Wrigley Field with my dad when I was probably no more than three years old.

My mom exuded warmth and support. A bit shy, she was much more inclined to hugs and kudos than Dad and, thus, a nice counterpoint to his sternness. After I began school at Emerson Elementary, a 19th-century brick edifice, she began teaching at another school in the nearby town of Broadview, where she was very popular with the students.

Having my father working in the same district where I attended school was a two-edged sword. On one hand, all the teachers treated me well—and maybe even made me something of a "teacher's pet"—because I was a principal's son. On the other hand, any misbehavior by me was quickly communicated to my dad, who was not averse to administering a little corporal punishment. So I was always motivated to be well-behaved, to do what I was told.

So strong was the pressure to behave that I can remember being punished only once while at Emerson. Some other kids and I were throwing rocks to try to dislodge a ball stuck in a tree on the playground. Somebody thought we were throwing rocks at the school windows. So we were marched into the principal's office and sternly reprimanded, our protestations notwithstanding. It wasn't a big deal, but I never got over what I thought was the injustice of being falsely accused. And decades later when I became a judge, I never forgot that lesson: Not everyone who gets hauled before the authorities is guilty.

Another benefit of being the son of educators was that I was taught to read before I began school. This gave me a leg up and contributed to academic success as I climbed the grades. Because my parents were both teachers, it was always understood that I would be a good student. I thought of myself as kind of a "cool" jock in junior high and high school. But I was also in what amounted to advance-placement classes, which others saw as nerdy.

Moving to Broadview

A lot of these opportunities stemmed from the fact that in the summer of 1952, when I was about nine, our family moved to the town of Broadview. For my parents, it was the fulfillment of the American Dream—a small, brick home with a yard in a better neighborhood. Though only a few miles southwest of Maywood, it was a solid middle-class community. What mattered to me was that it involved new friends, new schools, new coaches, and new opportunities. Life improved in practically every way. In fact, I would have to call it a turning point that profoundly, and positively, affected the rest of my life.

Attending Wilson Elementary School for fourth through sixth grades meant more and better chances. I played center field on the Broadview Little League All-Star Team, made new friends, and generally began to feel that I was leading a blessed life. (That sense of being guided by God has continued throughout my lifetime. I believe there's a primal force in the universe that, if we can listen to it and act upon it, will give us many of the answers we seek. Sadly, most people don't let it in.)

At Wilson, I also learned more of what I was capable of. Asked in the fifth grade to take the lead in the school play—a musical version of "The Pied Piper of Hamelin"—I was unsure of myself. Me, *sing*? But it turned out to be a big success for the school and a big confidence-builder for me.

The Eisenhower Expressway, now the main link between downtown Chicago and the communities to the west, was being built during much of my youth in Broadview. Lawsuits and other problems delayed the construction for years. That was bad for commuters but good for kids along the route. We sailed toy boats in the huge, rain-filled puddles left behind by the bulldozers. We dug for "gold" in the big mounds of dirt and debris. And once the highway was completed but not yet open, we rode bikes and roller-skated on the seemingly endless ribbons of concrete.

So that change of neighborhoods was another lucky break, of which I've had several in my life. Because if we'd stayed in Maywood, I probably would have gone to different schools and developed less confidence and self-esteem. It also felt good to move into a modest home with a yard instead of living in that cramped apartment. The Murphys had arrived in Middle America! It was a small step for us, but a good one.

Encouraged by my father, I also took a strong interest in sports and count some of my coaches as among my finest role models. One of them, Ray Meath, the baseball and basketball coach at Roosevelt Junior High, taught me many things, including the value of mentors. He took a liking to me early on and was wonderfully encouraging. No matter how poorly I played, he told me I could be great. His special interest in helping me develop my potential as an athlete was a huge blessing and, in turn, greatly enhanced my self-esteem. My athletic success encouraged me to run for eighth-grade president. After delivering a speech that my dad helped me write, I won the election and took my first step on the path of politics. (Ray and I still stay in touch all these decades later. He even attended my induction into the Proviso West High School Hall of Fame in 2001.)

Proviso West's First Graduate

My freshman year I attended the old, depressing Proviso East High School in Maywood. Due to the explosive post-war growth of Chicago's western suburbs, the high school was bursting at the seams with more than 5,000 students. My Spanish class, for instance, was held in the faculty lunchroom.

But once again, God smiled on me. At the start of my sophomore year, the township opened a brand-new second high school in Hillside, Illinois—Proviso West High School. Only freshman and sophomores were allowed to enroll at the new campus. Because our class would be the first to graduate from the new high school, the class of 1961 had the privilege of starting many of the school traditions.

A smaller high school with no juniors or seniors also provided me with a unique opportunity to play varsity sports. In addition to basketball, I ran on the varsity cross-country team and played varsity baseball.

Basketball fervor in Illinois at that time was almost indescribably high. If you saw the 1986 film *Hoosiers* about a small-town Indiana high school team in the 1950s that wins the state championship, you may have a sense of the fervor in neighboring Illinois as well. The passion and the pressure were intense. Even for a junior high game, hundreds of fans would crowd into the gym.

Our eighth grade team coached by Ray Meath, for example, had a 25-2 record and played all over the west Chicago suburbs. Jimmy Rodgers, a guy I played against during this time, went on to play professionally and coach the Boston Celtics and the Minnesota Timberwolves.

*All-conference forward Dick Murphy shoots at Proviso West High School
basketball game (1961)*

And high school basketball was even more spirited. Joe Hartley, our
coach, put me in the starting lineup as a sophomore. I think he liked my
positive attitude and obedient manner. My personal best that year on the
basketball court? When I scored 40 points against rival Oak Park High.
This feat (made possible by helpful assists from my long-time friend and
teammate Wolfgang Meister) won me a splash in the school paper and
even an announcement over the campus public-address system.

My senior year I led the team in scoring and assists and was selected
All-League First Team. I did the usual kinds of extracurricular activities
in high school, including dating a fair amount and being elected to the

Student Council. But a bigger change may have been happening beneath the surface: Until about age 14, I wanted to be a great athlete. After that, my dream was to make an impact on society.

One of my most significant lessons did not come in the classroom or on the basketball court. Having been elected student council vice president in my junior year of high school, I decided to run for senior class president. That goal held special significance because senior class presidents traditionally received the first diploma at graduation ceremonies. Thus, to win that election would mean becoming the very first graduate of Proviso West High School.

Unlike my campaign for student council vice president, the election for senior class president was hotly contested. All the candidates were to deliver an Election Day speech to the senior class, which numbered about 500. I had written a somewhat uninspiring speech about why I was best qualified to be senior class president. But divine providence intervened.

A few days before the election, my high school speech teacher, Paul Johnson, offered to help me with my delivery. After hearing the speech, though, he told me it was a loser. Mr. Johnson explained that voters wanted to know what I would do *for them* in the future, not what I had accomplished in the past. This 180-degree change of focus was an epiphany.

So we rewrote the speech. I won the election and became the first graduate of Proviso West. More important, I never forgot the simple life lesson: Whether you are pursuing a job, a spouse, or an election, the most important selling point is always what you can do for the *other* person.

Family Life

Our small family led a good, if simple, life. We were spiritual, though hardly doctrinaire. My parents drank only a little and then only when with friends. Due perhaps in large part to Mom's easygoing nature, family arguments were few and mild. Clear household rules were stated and enforced—no TV on school nights, no friends over when my parents were gone, a limit of one Coke per day. And vacations were frequent but Spartan: We'd usually go to southern Illinois, where both my parents hailed from and had relatives. My cousins and I caught fireflies there, jumped on grandma's big, flouncy bed, and just hung out during the long, hot, humid Midwestern summers. Other times we rented a lakeside cabin in Wisconsin or Indiana, or drove to Michigan to see the sights.

Hard work was never a stranger. My father, a bit of an authoritarian, made sure that every Saturday I mowed the lawn, raked the leaves, or shoveled snow. I also had a weekly paper route from the fifth through the 11th grade, and in the summers I worked as a bag boy at a local market.

My dad may have overdone it a bit. For instance, he insisted that each year I sell 225 bags of Halloween candy door-to-door to raise the $75 needed to go to Boy Scout camp. That was an ordeal, and I think he probably could have afforded the camp fee without my having to routinely pester the neighbors. But from his Depression-era perspective, working and saving were essential, like breathing. After all, that was how you learned to appreciate money. And, from where I sit now, I see that there are clearly worse fates. And if nothing else, the experience led me to be a little more lenient with my own kids.

Dad, as I mentioned, wasn't a terribly affectionate man. In fact, I—and probably most people—were a little afraid of him. But what he lacked in warm-fuzzy feelings, he sought to make up for in attentiveness. He would, for instance, come home daily at noontime to make lunch for me. On weekends, we'd shoot baskets together. (He was particularly intent on my learning to be a good free-thrower. As a result, I attained a respectable 80 percent accuracy at the foul lines in my high school games.) And believing that every man should be skilled at ballroom dance, he insisted I take lessons. He even arranged for me to endure three years of violin lessons with the music teacher at his school.

In short, my adolescence went by swimmingly. Though I might have yearned for a larger family, I knew our trio was solid. I got good grades, became senior class president, was named Most Valuable Player on the basketball team, and had an active social life. I even got to use the family car on weekends, provided I got home by 1 a.m.

My time in high school was wonderful, made more so by the fact that ours was the first graduating class in a brand-new campus. I was sad when my high school years were over because I thought life would never get any better than that. But I was wrong.

Alpha Tau Omega fraternity officers (1965)

2

THE COLLEGE YEARS:
Illinois and Harvard

"Two roads diverged in a wood, and I—
I took the one less traveled by,
And that has made all the difference."
—Robert Frost

IN THE FALL OF 1961, following in the footsteps of my parents, I enrolled as a freshman at the University of Illinois in Champaign-Urbana. This was still an era of simple academic and social pursuits. Yes, the 1960s had dawned, but the decade didn't yet ring with the cacophony of an unpopular war, racial strife, massive protests, assassinations, and the resultant cries of a bitterly divided nation. John F. Kennedy had just been elected president, and the country felt challenged but vigorous, young but strong. And so did I.

Choosing to attend U of I wasn't a tough decision. It seemed more academically oriented and less vocational than many other Illinois colleges. And the in-state tuition was $100 a semester, not a small factor for a family of modest circumstances. So for a number of those of us from Proviso West—middle class but unlikely candidates for Harvard or Yale—Illinois was a logical choice.

My dad wanted me to major in business administration, which he saw as leading to a stable and useful vocation. But I was more inclined toward liberal arts, such as political science and history. So we compromised: I'd enroll in the liberal arts college at the university, so I could take my poly sci and history classes, but major in economics.

A new era was dawning—the Peace Corps, space exploration, the first stirrings of civil rights, and other sweeping national ideas and causes. While I found those times exciting, I was really focused on being a good student and was mainly interested in local campus issues. I studied fairly hard, never missed a class, developed a good system for taking notes and cramming for tests, all good enough to help me be elected to Phi Beta Kappa. However, I did my best to balance academic and social life, and now look back on my college years as pretty good times.

Illinois Fraternity Life

Fraternities were very big at the University of Illinois, sometimes then referred to as the "frat capital of the world." Wanting to be cool, I pledged Alpha Tau Omega (ATO) during my freshman year because it was one of the most prominent of the 57 fraternity chapters at Champaign-Urbana. It was also akin to "Animal House," filled with varsity athletes and accomplished hell-raisers. Still thinking of myself as a jock (though not good enough to play at the Big Ten level), I lived at the house for four years with college athletes as roommates and some other pretty rowdy guys as fraternity brothers.

The ATO house was a wild and crazy place. Most of the fellows were into playing sports, drinking beer, and chasing women. I was a little more grounded than many of my housemates. But while enjoying much of the frivolity, I also learned from some of my frat brothers. For instance, Don Snodgrass, the chapter president and two years ahead of me, became yet another valuable mentor when he kind of took me on as a project. He counseled me to change my hair—get rid of the flattop, he urged—and pay more attention to how I dressed, and generally, to shape up and improve my image. It must have worked—I was eventually elected president of the fraternity chapter as well as to a seat on the Inter-Fraternity Council.

Social life was a major focus. I dated a fair amount, and in fact, was put on an annual list of "The 10 Most Eligible Bachelors on Campus" that ran on the front page of the school newspaper. Though I was proud of the honor at the time, it really meant that I didn't have a girlfriend.

Fun was found mostly in the frat parties and listening to the great rock 'n' roll and folk-rock of the time. In fact, that's still an interest of mine that, I think, surprises friends when they learn I've attended concerts by groups such as 10,000 Maniacs, the Eagles, and Counting Crows. (A slight digression: In middle age, when I was running for mayor, San Diego public radio station KPBS asked me and my opponent Ron Roberts to name our favorite songs of all time. I had no trouble reeling off one for each decade: Buddy Holly's "Peggy Sue" (1950s), Bob Dylan's and Peter, Paul and Mary's "Blowing in the Wind (1960s), the Eagles' "Peaceful, Easy Feeling" (1970s), Bruce Springsteen's "My Hometown" (1980s), and the Counting Crows' "A Long December" (1990s). After the election, one woman told me she'd voted for me solely on the basis of the music I'd listed in that interview.)

The fraternity wasn't all about hijinks, though. In fact, some of my most intense learning experiences sprang from my role as a chapter leader. I learned to run the organization and mediate disputes among its 100 members by, for example, working to quell clashes between members who wanted to party all the time and those who needed a quieter environment for studying.

ATO-Worthy Master

A particularly defining experience came as part of my frat role, though it happened far from campus. Near the end of my junior year, the fraternity members elected me president (aka "Worthy Master") for my senior year. One of my best friends, Bob ("Bates") Linn, was elected treasurer. As 21-year-olds, we'd been entrusted with the future of our fraternity chapter.

At the end of the school year, the national fraternity organization notified our local chapter that we were going to be placed on probation for a year due to our members' poor grades. Not only did that mean no social events for a house of party animals, it meant a major embarrassment that threatened to affect the chapter's image on campus and its ability to attract new members.

Our only hope was an appeal at the national fraternity convention that summer. It was no ordinary convention, however. It was the start of the 100-year anniversary celebration of the founding of Alpha Tau Omega. The national convention was to be held in the Bahamas.

Further underscoring this convention's historic role was the fact that the agenda contained a controversial resolution to repeal the national fraternity's century-old policy of limiting fraternity membership to white male Christians. For a fraternity founded in the South at the end of the Civil War, this would be a big step. Needless to say, our local chapter's issue was not very high on the agenda.

Just attending the convention proved logistically challenging for Bates and me during that summer of 1964. We drove an old car from Chicago to Miami. Just as we were about to board a boat for the Bahamas, a major hurricane struck. Our departure was delayed, and we had to spend the night in a Miami Beach hotel. Hundred-mile-an-hour winds soon blew out the hotel's upper-story windows, scattering shards of glass in all directions. The guests were all herded into the hotel lobby bar for an all-night vigil (which included unlimited free drinks).

When the eye of the storm passed over us, Bates decided he wanted to go for a swim in the ocean. Bad idea, I thought. But, then, I'd had a lot less to drink than he had. So I kept an eye on him as he achieved his dubious objective of swimming in the Atlantic during a hurricane.

Eventually arriving in the Bahamas for the national convention, we still faced a daunting challenge: A pair of 21-year-olds seeking to persuade the fraternity's national leadership to rescind our chapter's academic probation. Remembering my high school speech teacher's admonition, we knew that just telling them how deserving our chapter was would not carry the day. We needed to figure out how making an exception for our chapter would benefit the leaders of the national fraternity.

Fortuitously, the national fraternity headquarters was located in the same town as the University of Illinois. At the appeal hearing, we pointed out to the national fraternity leaders that many people would visit the national headquarters during the centennial year and some would want to visit our local chapter house. We convinced them that it would embarrass the national fraternity president and its executive director if the local chapter in the hometown of the national fraternity headquarters was on academic probation during the centennial celebration.

I was a bit apprehensive. This was a big challenge. But I've never minded making a speech if I have something worthwhile to say. And in this case, we had an argument of consequence. By then, my former speech teacher's advice about gearing your remarks toward the audience, instead of yourself, was automatic. So we passionately made the case about the Illinois chapter being a showcase for the national organization.

Miraculously, the national fraternity granted our appeal. The academic probation was rescinded. We were given another year to improve the local fraternity chapter's grade-point average, which we accomplished by assembling an especially smart pledge class. The lesson learned was that you can get people to do what you want if you can convince them that it meets their needs. And once again, I felt the hand of God had shown me the way.

By the way, the ATO national convention also did vote to repeal its policy limiting fraternity membership to white Christians. I was proud to cast the vote on behalf of the Illinois chapter in favor of the repeal. And in the fall of 1964, our chapter pledged its first Jewish member.

Summers at IBM

Another case where I believe God was looking out for me—because it became a life-changing experience—was being chosen as one of 16 high school grads to participate in a special IBM program called "Operation Cradle." The company had selected one graduating senior from each of the 16 academically strongest high schools in the Chicago suburbs. (Though the ultimate objective clearly was to develop future employees for IBM, ironically, only one of the 16 became a full-time employee. Most of the others eventually took other paths, such as going to medical school or earning a doctorate.) In the summer of 1961, we took five weeks' training in downtown Chicago where we learned to program nascent IBM computers that processed punch cards. Then we were put to work helping IBM's small business clients implement their data-processing systems.

I did that for five consecutive summers, all through my college years, and it was terrific—a great job that paid pretty well in a rapidly emerging and important field. What's more, the 16 of us became fast friends—almost like a fraternity of geeks—and would hang out together and hold weekend beach parties as we met for training at the start of every summer.

So, in effect, during those university years, I had two different sets of friends—the ATO jocks and party animals during the school year and the cerebral IBMers during the summer. Having that IBM experience—my only real contact with the business world—paid dividends in other ways, too. In fact, it'd be hard to over-estimate the role that has played in my life. Without it, I probably wouldn't have gotten into Harvard Business School or been assigned to the Army War Room at the Pentagon.

But the good times passed all too quickly. I graduated from the University of Illinois in June 1965, with a BA in Economics.

Harvard Business School

The choice then became, what next? Dad, as I mentioned, wanted me to go into business, or failing that, into teaching. Though I leaned toward law school, I applied to both law schools and graduate business schools. When Harvard Business School offered me a tuition scholarship that made the decision simpler.

In the fall of 1965, I enrolled at Harvard Business School, the so-called "West Point of Capitalism." The nation had changed during my

Harvard Business School graduation (1967)

four years at the University of Illinois. JFK's assassination had turned the Baby Boomers' idealism to cynicism. Dissension over civil rights has risen to the fore. And a politically unpopular war in Vietnam had begun to spark protests on college campuses.

Harvard Business School, on the other hand, remained remarkably insulated from the growing tide of discontent. Most of my fellow students were older than I and had previously worked in business or served in the military. Though not particularly snobbish, they were in many cases supremely confident and accomplished, having come from wealthy families and graduated from prestigious private schools. So they had a certain swagger that I probably lacked.

A number of them had worked for big accounting or consulting firms, or were the scions of powerful industrialists. In fact, in one of our Harvard case studies we read about an incident in which President Kennedy personally called the president of U.S. Steel to warn him against a price increase. One of my classmates was the son of that U.S. Steel chief.

Unlike many of my HBS classmates, my only previous business experience had been those summers working as a computer programmer and systems analyst at IBM. So I felt a bit like an outsider at first. It turned out, though, that my rich classmates from powerful families were not much different from the rest of us. And after the first semester, when it became clear I was doing better academically than many others, I felt more confident about my place there. I had learned that hard work and persistence can trump pedigree and wealth.

The schoolwork was somewhat arduous, especially the first year, because we went to class five or six days a week and had to submit a paper every other Saturday. And the HBS professors seemed to relish using the Socratic case-study method to intimidate students, straight out of the movie, *The Paper Chase*. But I did OK, made some great friends, and in general, found Harvard to be a good personal experience, though perhaps not a terrific vocational one. My heart still tugged me toward the law. In spite of my initial misgivings, I eventually graduated with a Master of Business Administration degree, ranking in the top third of the class.

Meeting Jan

But my singularly most significant achievement at HBS was meeting and courting my future wife, Janice Irene Cole. Jan had grown up in Holliston, Massachusetts, and had just graduated from the University of Connecticut with a B.S. in physical therapy. She was working as a

Jan and I, dating days (1966)

physical therapist at Massachusetts General Hospital, the teaching hospital for Harvard Medical School.

Harvard Medical School, which had mostly male students in those days, had invited all the female nurses and therapists who worked at Mass General to a mixer. My roommate and good friend Paul Echenberg and I decided to crash the mixer, pretending to be Harvard Medical School students. When Jan and I first met, my future bride was not too impressed, especially when she found out I was not going to be a physician. She wouldn't give me her phone number, but eventually I found it on my own. I had to do some fancy talking for an hour to get that first date. But my persistence and patience eventually won her over. And once we had that first date, we got along swimmingly. (In fact, I later learned that after that first date she told her roommate I was the guy she expected to marry.)

I was drawn to Jan, a pretty five-foot-one blonde, from the very beginning. She was both attractive and nice, virtues that I had found to be mutually exclusive in a lot of other women at that time. And she was a joy to get along with. If there'd been an eHarmony then, it would have probably matched us because we had similar philosophies, politics, and religious backgrounds. And, in fact, also parallel biographies in some ways: I'd been captain of the basketball team; she'd been captain of the cheerleading squad. Both of us had been senior class officers in our high school and played varsity sports (softball and basketball for her).

We had a wonderful courtship, enjoying many good times and trips throughout New England. We went to the Boston Pops, visited historic sites in Lexington and Concord, sailed on the Charles River, skied at Stowe in Vermont, biked around Martha's Vineyard, and water-skied while at Jan's parents' lakeside summer home in Maine.

During my second and final year at HBS, the focus of most students was on landing high-paying Wall Street jobs or at similar prestigious institutions. I opted instead to take a commission as an officer in the

United States Army. I was offered a second lieutenant's commission if I underwent just nine weeks' training, followed by a two-year active-duty obligation. The Army didn't make any promises about assignments, but suggested it would try to make use of my computer skills and business school experience. It was the "road less traveled by" HBS graduates, but—as Frost's poem says—the one "that has made all the difference."

United States Army Lieutenant (1967–1969)

3

THE UNITED STATES ARMY:
Inside the Pentagon
and the White House

"All we have to decide is what to do with the time that is given us."
—J.R.R. Tolkien

THE LATE 1960S WAS A FASCINATING PERIOD in America. An unpopular war was raging in Vietnam. The strident culture of dissent was starting to spread rapidly. But I'd been so busy getting an education during the early and mid-1960s that I hadn't been immersed in the political tumult of the times.

Sure, I greatly enjoyed some of the era's protest songs such as Peter, Paul and Mary's "Blowing in the Wind," the Kingston Trio's "Where Have All the Flowers Gone?" and Dion's "Abraham, Martin, and John." But I wasn't part of the pot-smoking, anti-war, anti-establishment hippie culture. I was exposed to it, but I wasn't dealing with it every day, so I wasn't really caught up in that militant fervor.

On the other hand, while I felt some patriotic duty, I wasn't thinking of the military as a career, either. I was thinking about how to best fulfill my military obligation, then get on with my yet-unfocused life.

So I sought a middle ground: become an officer and perhaps put my computer skills and schooling to use.

As it turned out, the Army and I in many ways were a good match. I was accustomed to following rules. In sports and in academics, I'd developed a "can-do" attitude that my teachers and coaches appreciated. So obeying military orders came somewhat naturally.

To receive my commission as an Army second lieutenant, I underwent nine weeks of training at Fort Benjamin Harrison in Indiana in the summer of 1967. The first three weeks were tough, but not so much after that. A cumulative score was needed to pass several physical training tests. Because I'd run cross-country in high school, I aced the running part (running a sub-six-minute mile in combat boots) and that earned me a good overall score. And the weapons training was actually kind of fun, almost like Boy Scout camp, except we were firing M-1s, M-16s, and .45-caliber pistols. The most challenging part of those first few weeks was the war games, where we had to crawl under barbed wire while live machinegun fire sprayed above us. That—as well as simulated treatment as a P.O.W.—was something to be endured.

But the academic training that dominated the rest of the course wasn't too tough, and I ended up class valedictorian. In fact, I was recruited by Army higher-ups to teach at Fort Benjamin Harrison. But I decided to take my chances with the regular Army assignment process—a gamble that paid off.

Inside the Pentagon

Upon completing training in September 1967, I was assigned to the Army Operations Center (also known as the Army War Room) at the Pentagon. I was excited about living in Washington, D.C., at such an historic time. What's more, the War Room—the nerve center for the Army's worldwide operations—was a particularly invigorating place to be. Much of my work related to top-secret projects that might still remain classified. I had several different assignments, primarily working with a team of civilians to develop software related to troop-deployment scenarios, such as this: With 500,000 U.S. troops in Vietnam, what ways could the Army choose to react if, say, Russia invaded West Germany, or China stormed Taiwan?

About a month after I arrived at the Pentagon, as many as 100,000 anti-war demonstrators protested outside the facility as U.S. involvement in Vietnam escalated. (I supported the war in Vietnam at that point, but later concluded that the cost in American lives had not been worth it. Meanwhile, I tolerated the dissenters but opposed the violent protests.)

While it wasn't the biggest protest of the era, the March on the Pentagon that day may have been the most historically significant because of the target. It's now seen as what the *Washington Post* called "a touchstone event in American history" in which U.S. citizens massed at the "high church of the military-industrial complex," as author Norman Mailer put it. The Pentagon was on high alert. Troops were stationed in and around it, and machine guns were set up in its hallways. The protest occurred on Saturday, Oct. 21, 1967. I was told to stay home that day and did, but watched the events with interest.

A few months later, God opened another door. I ran into a White House speechwriter at a Harvard Business School party. To this day I'm not sure why he was so helpful; we'd just met. Regardless, he told me about an opening for a White House "military social aide" and gave me a phone number.

I was invited to the White House to meet with the President's chief military aide, and landed one of the two available jobs. I still worked at the Pentagon, so this was extra duty, but it was *great* extra duty. After all, I got to mingle with kings and prime ministers as well as Congressional leaders, cabinet secretaries, Supreme Court justices, and the Presidents and their families.

Why was I chosen? Maybe because I already had a Top Secret clearance and worked at the Pentagon. Perhaps because I was single and thus could act as an escort. And probably the Harvard Business School degree didn't hurt. In any event, I was again fortunate to be at the right place at the right time.

Inside the White House

While I continued to work full time in the Army War Room, I typically would be assigned 10 to 15 additional hours each week at the White House as one of a dozen-plus aides from all five branches of the military. Our interactions with the President and the First Lady were frequent, but almost always brief and in the line of duty.

The President often hosted state dinners or receptions for the leaders of foreign nations. Most of the aides would be assigned to such events. At times I would be in charge of the receiving line for the President and the visiting head of state and would officially announce each guest. At other times, I would be assigned to escort special guests. (For example, I was assigned to King Constantine of Greece at the reception for foreign heads of state after President Eisenhower's funeral.) We were to introduce them to various dignitaries whom we were trained to recognize.

Many times the guests we escorted were unmarried women, thus the nickname for the military social aides was the "White House gigolos." Among those I escorted were Peggy Fleming, the Olympic skating champion; Baroness Maria Von Trapp, who was the inspiration for *The Sound of Music*; and iconic White House reporter Helen Thomas.

At least one of the aides would be assigned to every ceremony at the White House. At military ceremonies, like awarding Medals of Honor, I would usually announce the President as he entered the room: "Ladies and Gentlemen, the President of the United States" (after musical fanfare).

President and Mrs. Lyndon Johnson with White House military aides (1968)

Another of my tasks was to hand the commemorative pens to the President during bill-signing ceremonies. I particularly remember attending the signing of the Civil Rights Act of 1968. Commonly known as the Fair Housing Act, it was meant as a follow-up to the Civil Rights Act of 1964 and prohibited housing discrimination on the grounds of race, color, religion, or national origin.

At swearing-in ceremonies for high-ranking government officials, I would sometimes sit with the honoree in an anteroom waiting for the cue to escort him or her to the East Room. Usually I would walk with the dignitaries to the reception area and announce their arrival so other guests could pay their proper respects. Then I'd normally fade into the background.

Among those I met in this capacity was Chief Justice Earl Warren, who was surprisingly humble and approachable. We spent five or ten minutes together, briefly discussing his experience as Chief Justice and my interest in the law.

My biggest concern at the White House was that I'd make a major faux pas. Unfortunately, the White House didn't use nametags in the 1960s. So as a memory aid, I kept track of who was who by making a mental note of the colors of the dresses worn by the male guests' wives. But one night the improbable happened—two ladies wore the exact same dress—and as a result, I introduced the chairman of the Joint Chiefs of Staff, who was in civilian clothes, as the president of Eastern Airlines. The general was not impressed, and he quickly—and sternly—corrected me. Although I suppose he could have easily gotten me fired over that, he didn't.

Presidential Family Observations

My roughly 18 months of White House service spanned the Lyndon Johnson and Richard Nixon presidencies, so I also got to see those two Presidents close up. I worked with President Johnson during his last year in office after he'd decided not to run for re-election in the face of mounting opposition to the Vietnam War. He often seemed tired and grumpy. Once when I was urging him to pose yet again for photos with visiting dignitaries, he sternly reminded me that he was Commander in Chief.

Lady Bird Johnson, on the other hand, was always pleasant and upbeat and was everyone's favorite. President Johnson's older daughter, Lynda Bird, was engaged to one of the White House military social aides, Chuck Robb, who was destined to become a U.S. senator from Virginia. The President's youngest daughter, Luci, was a fun-loving free spirit who would often dance with me and the other young aides at state dinners.

When I served in the first six months of the Nixon Administration, I found President Nixon to be a little stiff and formal, but he went out of his way to be cordial to the military aides. Shortly after his election, he even hosted a reception for all of the military aides in the family living quarters upstairs at the White House.

First Lady Pat Nixon appeared shy and uncomfortable in her role, but nevertheless continued the tradition of working with the White House military social aides to host small receptions at the White House. President Nixon's daughter, Julie, who was married to President Eisenhower's grandson, David, was very personable and outgoing. The President's other daughter, Tricia, was the prettiest of the four presidential daughters I met, but was always quiet and aloof.

The First Ladies would often host small receptions at the White House for groups such as the Daughters of the American Revolution. An aide would always be assigned to assist the First Lady. I would typically meet the First Lady, escort her to the reception, announce her arrival, and organize a receiving line. Young male military aides in uniform were always popular with the older ladies at these events.

Occasionally the aides would be assigned duties with the First Family away from the White House. For example, each of us was assigned (with a date) to attend one of the Inaugural Balls in January of 1969 and to

President and Mrs. Richard Nixon with White House military aides (1969)

officially announce the arrival of President Nixon at the event. And I also escorted Tricia Nixon when she was queen of the Azalea Festival in Norfolk, Virginia. Of course, we only spent time together at official events. Actually, I hung out more with the Secret Service agents at the festival than with Tricia.

I was kind of awestruck by these celebrities at first. But after a while, I got over it when I saw that they, for the most part, were just ordinary people in extraordinary roles. As I got to know many of them at least in passing, it became clear that they owed their rise more to perseverance and luck than overwhelming talent. And that reinforced my belief that so much of our lives hinge on a good attitude mated with good fortune.

What's more, being around all these important people also put my own sense of self into perspective by showing me where I was in the pecking order. (When the presidency passed from Johnson to Nixon, the butlers, the cooks, and the military social aides were the only staffers who were carried over into the next administration. What does *that* tell you?)

Between the two jobs—the Pentagon during the day and the White House at night—I was probably working 60 hours a week without extra pay. But it was a great gig!

Though the combined hours at the Pentagon and the White House were long, I still managed to have some diversions. Norm McClave, a fellow soldier who was also a buddy from Harvard Business School, acted as kind of an unofficial tour guide. Like me, he was especially interested in history, so we—Jan and I and Norm and his girlfriend— explored a number of Civil War battlefields together and hiked along the old Chesapeake & Ohio Canal as well as took in the Army-Navy football game in Philadelphia.

Another time my Army roommates and I decided to hitch a ride on a military plane to Central and South America. Because the plane—a loud, slow cargo transport—flew a scheduled weekly route, we were going to make stops in the Canal Zone, Rio de Janeiro, and Trinidad. But on the leg from Panama to Rio, one of the plane's flaps malfunctioned, forcing us into an unscheduled week-long stay in the town of Paramaribo, in Suriname, the former Dutch Guiana just north of Brazil. We stayed in a fleabag hotel, explored the town, and made friends with the young Dutch people who ran the bauxite mines there. This was my first experience in a Third World country. We did eventually make it to Rio.

Setting Priorities

Those Pentagon-White House years (1967–1969) convinced me that just about any career goal was possible. I sensed that those who had clear aims and worked hard generally did pretty well. And, specifically, living and working in Washington underscored my latent interest in law and government; I could see that what the people there were doing was both worthwhile and interesting.

I had enjoyed college history classes very much and hadn't yet totally given up on the idea of becoming a history professor. But once I'd seen history being made—such as the March on the Pentagon and the signing of epic legislation—I knew that teaching and writing about events wouldn't be nearly as interesting as being a part of them, however minor a part that might be.

But when I got out of the Army in 1969, I still wasn't clear about what exactly I wanted to do. If I could have articulated my priorities at the time, they likely would have looked something like this:

- Get married and have a family.
- Gain some financial security.
- Make a contribution to society.

I knew I wanted Jan to be my partner for my marriage and family goal. But I was still a little hazy on details related to the other two. Filled with optimism, yes. Imbued with energy, definitely. But like the character Benjamin Braddock in the movie *The Graduate*, I remained vague on just *how* I was going to make a difference.

Murphy Family—Brian, Dick, Shannon, Jan, Kelly (1980)

4

Career Decisions:
Business, Law, or Politics?

"It's never too late to be what you might have been."
—*George Elliott*

My White House experience had been terrific because of the people I'd met and the events I'd witnessed. The Pentagon assignment had been great because of the insights it gave me on how to survive in a large, structured organization. And the Army computer exposure was, well, interesting.

I'd already decided I didn't want a career in computers. But what I found was that the time in Washington had rekindled my latent interest in law and government, though I was unsure how to pursue it. I probably could've stayed there and worked on Capitol Hill, but that didn't excite me. I'd matured a lot in the Army and thus was ready when—in the span of just about a month in 1969—my life underwent some major changes:

- July 4—I got out of the Army
- July 19—Jan and I were married
- August 1—Jan and I joined a political campaign

By the time I'd left active duty as an Army officer, Jan and I had been dating nearly three years. We were married in the Martha Mary Chapel at Longfellow's Wayside Inn in South Sudbury, Massachusetts, on July 19, 1969. The next day many of our young friends joined us on our honeymoon at Jan's parents' vacation home in Maine, where we saw man's first step on the moon. That was an auspicious beginning to our own journey, which would be filled with many surprises.

An Historic Election

Linwood Holton was the Republican candidate for governor of Virginia, a moderate whose principles I could feel comfortable with. I'd have to admit I wasn't at that point an impassioned voter or a committed Republican. So while joining his campaign may have been kind of rash, I needed to do something while figuring out what I was really going to do with my life.

I'd struck up a friendship with Holton at the Azalea Festival where I'd escorted Tricia Nixon. He asked me to be the deputy campaign manager in charge of scheduling. Another fortuitous opportunity! And another reason to believe that God had a plan for me. Though I didn't know what that plan was, I kept seeing doors opening and I kept going through them.

Not that it was a perfect fit. Although I felt comfortable with Holton's philosophy, being a Yankee working in Richmond for a Virginia gubernatorial candidate meant that some people saw us as carpetbaggers. About three-fourths of the staffers were from out of state, a fact that the press and the Democratic candidate pointed out with delight.

Meanwhile, Jan, who'd reluctantly signed on to manage Holton's state campaign headquarters, was being run ragged. It was a miserable experience for her, a total immersion in the minutiae of campaigning: manning the phones, answering staff and voter complaints, dealing with the mail. We'd been married only two weeks, so this was a real test of her loyalty. But she learned a lot about politics in a short time, which might be why she never again worked in another campaign (except for mine).

However, we got what we bargained for—an interesting, challenging, and exhausting opportunity to see a political campaign up close. What's more, it turned out to be an historic election. In November 1969 Linwood Holton became the first Republican elected governor of Virginia since Reconstruction. It was the beginning of the Democratic South turning Republican and the great geographical political realignment of America.

When Holton won, I was offered a job with the new governor's administration. But I wasn't seriously tempted. We still felt like carpet-baggers and decided that working in Richmond wasn't the right fit for us.

But if not that, *what?*

Moving to San Diego

I still hadn't figured out my career path. Jan's vocation as a physical therapist, though, was solid and could be practiced almost anywhere. So we decided to move someplace we really wanted to be... and let the jobs flow from that decision. We knew we didn't want to live in D.C. Boston, where Jan was from, didn't appeal to me, and I didn't want to go back to the frigid Chicago winters.

Then we saw a favorable article in *National Geographic* about San Diego's 200th birthday—bingo! In December 1969 we packed our meager belongings into our 1965 Chevy Nova, left Richmond, and headed west. We tried camping out along a southern route, but soon found out that the South also had chilly winter nights.

Despite the fact that neither of us had ever been there and didn't know a soul in the area, San Diego pretty much fulfilled our expectations. It featured the ocean and beautiful beaches, interesting topography (compared, at least, to Illinois), a wonderful climate, and in general, seemed like a good combination of big-city living and small-town values. And San Diegans were very welcoming, unlike some Virginians.

It seemed friendly and laid-back and not all that different from the Midwest. Pete Wilson, who hailed from Illinois, was running for mayor. And other Midwestern transplants were numerous. (In fact, some years later, when I first ran for mayor, enough alumni from my high school lived in San Diego to throw a party for me there.)

Bank of America

We took up residence in an Ocean Beach cottage for $95 a month, and after three months of playing golf and tennis and hanging out at the beach, Jan and I both nailed down jobs. First, she was hired by Children's Hospital as a pediatric physical therapist. That put the pressure on me.

Because I had an MBA, I thought I should at least try to get a job in business, and what's more business-like than a bank? So when Bank of America offered me a newly created position of San Diego Regional Marketing Officer, I jumped at it. This came at a time when B of A was trying to enhance its image after anti-war protesters burned down its Isla Vista branch, about 250 miles north, in Santa Barbara. I served on a task force to advise Bank of America higher-ups how to respond to that crisis. I reported to the San Diego regional vice president, but because I also advised the national marketing director, I got even more visibility within the company.

Interestingly, I was kind of the "kid" in the B of A office. I was still in my twenties, while many of the managers were in their forties and the big bosses in their fifties. So they kind of "adopted" me—the new kid with the fresh ideas. All of which made working there an especially fun experience.

We loved San Diego in the early 1970s, which we found to be an attractive big city with a friendly, small-town atmosphere. Before long,

Jan and I moved to an apartment near Children's Hospital (so she could walk to work and we could get by on our one car). I dabbled a little bit in San Diego politics: supporting Pete Wilson's first election as mayor in 1971 and getting elected myself to the San Diego County Republican Central Committee. And best of all, our first child, Brian, was born at Mercy Hospital in the spring of 1972. Life was good.

Still, I kept feeling the call to pursue a career in law.

I liked working at B of A. And, in fact, I was offered a job as chief aide to the senior vice president in charge of all of California. That would've been a great job, but I turned it down because I didn't want to accept it and then quit to go to law school. It was becoming clear that I needed to do what I should have done five or six years earlier—follow through on my yearnings and go to law school. It was time to do what I *really* wanted to do.

Of course, we had a four-month-old baby at the time, and though supportive, Jan was probably weary of my career meanderings. My father was also fit to be tied about my leaving a promising business career to attend law school. But I knew I had to roll the dice in what I now see as kind of a gutsy move. I believe it is best to take chances in life. Trying and failing is better than regretting never having tried.

Stanford Law School

I applied and was accepted at Stanford Law School in the fall 1972. In the early 1970s, Stanford University was a hotbed of liberal activism, especially among idealistic law students who were bent on saving the world. Needless to say, few of my new classmates joined me in voting for President Nixon in his 1972 re-election campaign. (The only other admitted Republican in my class was Peter Ehrlichman, son of John Ehrlichman, one of President Nixon's chief advisors.) I felt a bit like a fish out of water, not because of being a Republican in a left-leaning school and region but because by now I was a married father and Vietnam-era veteran, while most of my fellow students were younger, unattached, and less experienced.

At the same time, it was a relaxed and friendly academic environment, an intellectually stimulating and culturally vibrant place. The students, such as Doug McGlashan, were generally supportive of one another, and the professors were friendlier and more approachable than those at Harvard had been. I especially liked Stanford Law School because I loved the subject matter. The classes—especially constitutional law and the new field of environmental law—were very engrossing. And the Stanford students were more cerebral as opposed to the smart, but more vocationally oriented students at Harvard Business School.

We lived in Escondido Village, Stanford University's on-campus housing for married graduate students with children. It was an international experience. Jan made many friends among the spouses of foreign grad

Stanford Law School (1975)

students. Our son Brian's playmates at Stanford's Bing Nursery School came from all over the world.

Leaving the corporate world to be a student meant that finances were tight. I received financial aid courtesy of the GI Bill and rode a bike to class from our housing complex. And Jan worked part-time as a physical therapist once Brian was in pre-school.

Living and going to school at Stanford was generally a very positive experience. Yet being a full-time student didn't give me too much time to play the daddy role. Like most first-time parents, Jan and I found the initial months with our first baby to be quite challenging. But, fortunately, Jan—whose years of babysitting for a younger sister had prepared her well—proved to be a great mom, and as we had more kids, I learned to be a better dad.

I graduated in June 1975, passed the bar exam on the first try, and was sworn in as an attorney on December 16, 1975—my 33rd birthday.

Judge T

After graduation, I was extraordinarily fortunate to land a position as a law clerk for U.S. District Judge Howard Turrentine in San Diego. He was a man of unparalleled integrity and legal scholarship who saw the training of law clerks as part of his job. He helped me to think like a lawyer and make decisions like a judge.

Judge T has been one of the most important mentors in my life, as he has been for many of his law clerks during his long tenure on the federal bench. A no-nonsense judge, he taught the art of fully studying a problem, then making a decision and moving on.

For a year I wrote legal memorandums along with fellow law clerks Kelly Edwards and Terry Shippen, making recommendations to the judge on both civil and criminal cases. After that year, I was hired by Luce, Forward, Hamilton, and Scripps, then San Diego's second biggest law firm.

With U.S. District Judge Howard Turrentine, for whom I was a law clerk

Luce, Forward

In the late 1970s, Luce, Forward was more like a fraternity than a business. Senior partners like Ed Luce, Bill McKenzie, and Bob Steiner took a genuine interest in teaching young associates how to be successful lawyers. Fellow associates like Bob Bell and Craig Andrews were supportive colleagues and good friends. The associates even put on skits making fun of senior partners without fear of reprisal.

Being an attorney at Luce, Forward also meant working on many interesting matters. For instance, I worked with senior partner Bob Steiner to successfully defend the San Diego Board of Realtors in an antitrust lawsuit alleging price fixing of real estate sales commissions. In that case, I took 50 depositions and analyzed some 10,000 documents. In another, I worked with senior partner Jerry Davee on behalf of the San Diego Zoo to prohibit Hare Krishnas from soliciting donations from zoo visitors. And as a member of the firm's recruiting committee, I traveled nationwide searching for talent to join the firm.

I spent almost five years at Luce, Forward, and the experience validated my belief that law was genuinely my field. I found the law to be inherently interesting. It paid well. My colleagues were terrific. I could have spent a career there.

Parenthood

While I was pursuing a career as an attorney, Jan and I were also making great strides as a family. We bought our first home on Deerfield Street in the San Carlos community of San Diego. Our first daughter, Shannon, was born in 1976. Our second daughter, Kelly, was born in 1979.

Despite my demanding work schedule, I tried hard to avoid being an absentee father. And I took to heart the message of "Cats in the Cradle," the folk-pop song by Harry Chapin in which the father is too busy to spend time with his son.

In my spare time, I began a run of coaching some 20 youth soccer, baseball, softball, and basketball teams on which my children played. (All three won multiple varsity letters in high school sports.) So as our children got older, I played an increasing role, not only teaching them sports and coaching their teams but also videotaping their plays and recitals, helping with homework, teaching them to drive, visiting prospective colleges with them, and doing all the other things that involved dads do. And our family made it a point to always eat dinner together.

I believe I was a less demanding father than my dad had been. But I did negotiate written "behavior contracts" with the kids in which their allowance and other perks depended on how well they behaved and did their chores. For example, they could lose money if they didn't make their beds or clean their rooms. They were given a car in high school if they got certain grades and if they didn't smoke or get tattoos. And although this system worked well, it also evoked some mild guffawing behind my back.

During my time at Luce, Forward, I also became active in the community. Mayor Pete Wilson appointed me to the San Diego Park and Recreation Board in 1978, and I became chairman two years later. I was appointed to the Mission Trails Regional Park Citizens Advisory Committee in 1979 and was again elected to the Republican Central Committee in 1980. But a more significant opportunity for public service was lurking and would soon present another difficult choice.

San Diego City Councilmember (1981–1985)

5

THE SAN DIEGO CITY COUNCIL:
The Best—and Worst—of Times

"It was the best of times, it was the worst of times."
—Charles Dickens, *A Tale of Two Cities*

DURING MY FIRST COUPLE OF YEARS at Luce, Forward, I just put my head down and worked very hard. But after that, though I continued to work hard, I began again to think about my long-term priorities. With regard to the first priority—marriage and a family—I was on track. On the second one, achieving a degree of financial security, I was seeing real progress. But the third one—making a contribution to society–well, perhaps that one needed a bit more attention.

So I asked Mayor Pete Wilson in 1978 to appoint me to the city Park and Recreation Board, which he was happy to do. I had a special interest in this area because the land that would eventually become part of Mission Trails Regional Park was near our home. In fact, we lived just a mile from the beautiful, rugged area known as Mission Gorge, where the San Diego River tumbles from the foothills toward central San Diego. This land was almost all privately owned at the time, and I was interested in preserving it for public use.

My hope was that as a member of that board, I could have a say in getting some of the city's $65 million of open-space bond-issue money spent on land acquisition in Mission Gorge. Plus, from coaching son Brian's soccer team, I also knew that this part of the city was lacking practice fields. So both those goals whetted my interest.

The appointment to the board seemed to be a good fit. The first year I chaired the City Lakes Subcommittee, which developed a plan for recreation on the eight city-owned reservoirs, which included nearby Lake Murray. The following year I was appointed vice chair of the Park & Rec Board as well as the board's representative to the Citizens Advisory Committee of the nascent Mission Trails Regional Park. And in 1980 I was appointed chair of the Park and Recreation Board and got involved in developing criteria for spending those open-space bond funds. I enjoyed serving on the board with many outstanding people, such as engineer Bill Rick, architect Hal Sadler, and Pete Wilson's future wife, Gayle. With their help and that of city staff, I was able to get the Mission Gorge area placed near the top of the list of the city's open-space-purchase priorities.

All this Park & Rec experience piqued my interest in local government and how it could improve residents' lives. Meanwhile, I'd joined the Republican Central Committee to network with local GOP activists. Then, in the spring of 1980, City Councilmember Larry Stirling, whose District 7 included our neighborhood, decided to run for State Assembly. That presented me with a tough choice when Pete Wilson and Stirling asked me to apply for an appointment to Stirling's old council seat if he won (he did).

City Council Appointment

All my Park and Recreation Board service was part-time and unpaid while I worked at Luce, Forward. But joining the city council would be a whole different ballgame—a full-time job with lots of responsibility, but about a 50 percent pay cut from what I earned at the law firm.

I'd been happy at Luce, Forward, was doing well, and was on track to become a partner, which potentially would assure my financial future. I particularly liked the other attorneys. The older lawyers were helpful, and the younger ones didn't appear to be fiercely competing with one another. So I knew I would feel bad about leaving them. And after having already tolerated my jettisoning a good job with Bank of America to attend law school, my wife was rightfully dubious about the possibility of my leaving Luce, Forward to join the city council.

On the other hand, she and I both recognized that an appointment to the city council could be a once-in-a-lifetime opportunity to hold a significant political office without having to campaign for it. And though I agonized over the decision, again it seemed as if God was opening a door.

I decided to go for it. After all, I reminded myself, Stirling might not win. And I might not get appointed. Even with Mayor Pete Wilson's support, the appointment was not a slam-dunk. To win the seat with Stirling gone, I needed five Yes votes from the eight remaining members of the city council. And after a long hearing in which the candidates were quizzed by the councilmembers, I eventually garnered the necessary five votes from Republican councilmembers Bill Mitchell, Bill Cleator, Bill Lowery, and Fred Schnaubelt along with the mayor. I was sworn in as the District 7 councilmember on December 16, 1980—my 38th birthday.

The Luce, Forward people were somewhat dismayed and, in truth, the move may not have been the smartest one for me financially. But I felt it was a natural evolution as well as an acknowledgment of the pull of public service. (In the back of my mind, I thought that if I didn't win the seat outright in the election less than a year later, I could return to Luce, Forward.)

Being sworn in as a councilmember by the city clerk as Mayor Pete Wilson looks on (1981)

City Council Election

The appointment was only for the duration of Stirling's elected term, which ended in December 1981. So there was no time to procrastinate. The euphoria of winning the appointment quickly turned into the reality of organizing an election campaign. (In the era before district-only elections, the primary election was held in the council district in September of odd-numbered years. The top two finishers in the district election met in a citywide runoff election two months later.)

I hired experienced staff, starting with John Kern, who'd been Stirling's city council chief of staff, and Carolyn Booth, who had run Stirling's council campaign. John helped get me up to speed on city issues, and Carolyn quickly put together a campaign organization to face my main opponent, Lucy Goldman.

Lucy was a liberal Democratic Party activist with strong ties to the Jewish community and the feminist movement. She and Pete Wilson were at odds because she'd been a key figure in the successful effort to defeat Wilson's proposed downtown convention center. She saw me as one of Pete's close allies.

Lucy had the money to run an aggressive campaign, and she sought to make our race a referendum on the mayor's downtown redevelopment plans. She ran television ads attacking my support for redevelopment and the proposed Horton Plaza Shopping Center development. However, our polling showed that a majority of San Diego voters supported downtown redevelopment and liked the proposed shopping center. So I felt a bit like B'rer Rabbit in the Uncle Remus folktale in which the rabbit convinces his antagonists to banish him to the brier patch, which was actually the place where he wants to be. (This, incidentally, meshes with my theory that most campaigns are actually lost by the other side rather than won by the victor.)

She *was* correct, of course. I was a big supporter of downtown redevelopment. As a councilmember, I would vote for Horton Plaza, the convention center, and other such projects, and when I now look at our vibrant, modern downtown, I'm especially proud of those stands.

It was a hard-fought campaign. I personally knocked on the doors of more than 10,000 registered voters in District 7, walking precincts nearly every weekday from 5 p.m. until dark and all day Saturday. I liked precinct walking. I would knock on voters' doors, introduce myself as their council representative, and ask if there was anything they needed from the City. Usually, they'd say no, I'd give them a brochure, and leave. But if they said yes—for instance, if a street light was out or a pothole needed to be filled—I'd get it taken care of. It was a wonderful way to find out what really mattered to voters. In fact, I kept knocking on doors even after I was elected. And sometimes, even to this day, residents tell me they remember my stopping by their houses years ago.

With Governor/Senator/Mayor Pete Wilson

Raising money wasn't nearly as pleasant. Giving a talk and chatting with guests at a fundraiser wasn't so bad, but I really didn't enjoy calling people to ask for money. However, with the help of Pete Wilson and Bill Cleator, we raised over $145,000 in campaign contributions, a record amount for a council race at the time. When it was all said and done, I finished first in the District 7 primary election in September and won the citywide runoff election in November with 53 percent of the vote.

The Best of Times

I felt fairly confident as a new councilmember because I'd already served a year and knew my goals: help create Mission Trails Regional Park and build other parks, streets, and libraries in District 7. Though I may still have had some doubts about a career in politics, I definitely was excited about having four more years on the council.

And, in fact, those first two years (1981–1982) were the best of times. Pete Wilson was mayor and a political ally. We dedicated the first San Diego trolley line from downtown San Diego to the Mexican border. We gave the go-ahead to construction of the Horton Plaza Shopping Center, which jump-started downtown redevelopment. We implemented the open-space bond act to acquire land for Mission Trails Regional Park and Los Penasquitos Canyon Preserve. And I was able to successfully initiate many worthwhile projects in my council district.

In the next chapter, I'll detail some of the citywide initiatives I'm particularly proud of. But, meanwhile, let me just note a few of the accomplishments in District 7. For instance, in the neighborhood of Tierrasanta, I focused on building much-needed infrastructure. A new library was constructed there. The first phase of Tierrasanta Community Park was completed. And the east end of Clairemont Mesa Boulevard was widened from two to four lanes, providing a level of access and egress that hadn't existed before.

In the College/Rolando community, I pursued reducing the impact of San Diego State University on the surrounding residential neighborhoods. The City implemented one of San Diego's first residential-permit parking districts, preventing SDSU students from parking in the surrounding residential neighborhoods. The City also adopted a fraternity overlay zone that limited the areas where fraternities and sororities could locate. And we built a city park on the playground of Hardy Elementary School, adjacent to SDSU.

In the Del Cerro, San Carlos, and Allied Gardens communities, we purchased Rancho Mission Canyon and built Rancho Mission Canyon Park as well as Princess Del Cerro Park and initiated phase one of the Lake Murray Community Park project. We expanded the Allied Gardens

Library from 4,000 to 6,500 square feet. And we extended Jackson Drive from Navajo Road to Mission Gorge Road.

Even though the pay was lousy and the hours were long, I was enjoying being a San Diego City councilmember. I liked all the other councilmembers. My council staff, headed by my long-time friend John Kern, was talented and dedicated. Even my somewhat skeptical wife was enjoying herself. For instance, during a volleyball exhibition fundraiser at San Diego State University, Jan presented a rose to heartthrob actor Tom Selleck on behalf of the women of San Diego and received a televised thank-you kiss from him.

The council job was turning out to be more fun and interesting—and it involved a more valuable contribution to society—than my work at Luce, Forward. So political life was even better than I expected, mainly because I was able to make such a big impact. But, alas, the good times did not last.

The Worst of Times

Change came to the council in November 1982, when Mayor Pete Wilson was elected to the U.S. Senate. I knew I would miss him, but at the time I didn't know how much of a loss that would be. What I found was that having had an ally in the mayor's office made getting things done much easier.

Deputy Mayor Bill Cleator became acting mayor pending a special election for mayor. The most notable event during Cleator's short time as acting mayor was a visit to San Diego from England's Queen Elizabeth. Cleator's incidental touching of the Queen during a reception caused some laughable criticism from the British press, which accused Cleator of fondling the Queen. In the special election for mayor in May 1983, San Diego County Supervisor Roger Hedgecock prevailed over Cleator and former councilmember Maureen O'Connor. I supported

Cleator out of loyalty. After all, he'd been one of the five votes for my original appointment to the council and he'd helped raise money for my 1981 race.

Hedgecock's election provoked a power struggle between Cleator and the new mayor. They particularly fought over appointments to boards and commissions, and I was caught in the middle. In truth, I didn't really care that much whether Hedgecock's liberal allies or Cleator's more conservative ones were appointed. But while I would've preferred to have an alliance with Hedgecock on some issues, I did feel I owed loyalty to Cleator. Unfortunately, the tussle over appointments soon spilled into other issues.

Roger's confrontational style exacerbated the conflict, polarizing the City Council into two warring factions. I'd known Hedgecock for more than a decade. We'd served on some of the same boards and shared similar positions about the environment. Though I knew he could be acerbic, I thought I would be able to work with him. I was wrong.

Our relationship didn't deteriorate immediately. For a while, Roger and I worked well together. We made several lobbying trips to Washington, D.C., and cooperated in the effort to build the San Diego Trolley's east line. What's more, I supported his effort to build a convention center.

But the mayoral election of 1984 brought the tension to a flashpoint. Hedgecock was running for reelection against Cleator-backed candidate Dick Carlson. I preferred Hedgecock because he was more qualified. However, he was also under investigation by the District Attorney's office for alleged campaign-finance irregularities. So I declined to endorse either candidate. Hedgecock won, and soon after he took office, the simmering power struggle with Cleator erupted into open warfare.

Hedgecock appeared to be intent on punishing those he considered his political enemies, including me. When I was out of town, he struck.

The post of deputy mayor had traditionally gone to the most senior councilmember who had not previously held the post, which would have been me in 1985. But while I was in Israel representing the City on a goodwill mission, Hedgecock lined up the enough council votes to elect Bill Mitchell as deputy mayor.

By 1985, the District Attorney was pursuing felony charges against Hedgecock. Councilmembers were jockeying to position themselves to succeed him if he was forced from office. The council had degenerated into a toxic environment where personal vendettas, political intrigue, and backstabbing took priority over the City's business. Instead of voting an issue up or down on its merits, councilmembers began voting based on who was, or was not, supporting a particular measure.

The best of times had become the worst of times on the San Diego City Council. I was still able to accomplish some things, such as small projects in my district, but the hostile council environment made the work much less enjoyable.

Moving On

Meanwhile, we were struggling a bit financially as a family. Trying to get by on half my Luce, Forward salary meant Jan had to go back to work part-time as a physical therapist at Children's Hospital. Brian and Shannon were in school, but daughter Kelly was in pre-school, and I occasionally needed to babysit her. So I'd take her to the office and also to political events once in a while. (Even as a tot, she had an ability to charm people, and years later showed her political chops by managing one of my mayoral campaigns.)

Being a city councilmember entails a 60- to 80-hour workweek when done diligently. In fact, I once calculated there are as many as 1,000 events a year that a councilmember could attend. To go to even a small fraction of them means a dearth of time for non-political friends or even for reflection. It's tough to find time to think about what you're doing and how you could do it better. The sense that you're in a never-ending marathon probably impedes optimal performance.

The spare time I did manage to wrest was spent enjoying my family and coaching my children's sports teams. We usually spent family vacations in Florida, where my parents and Jan's widowed mother had moved. And I did get to travel on council business. For instance, I went with a group of elected officials from California to inspect trash-to-energy plants and mass transit in France, Germany, and Switzerland. The San Diego United Jewish Federation took a group of San Diego elected officials on a particularly fruitful trip to Egypt and Israel, where I came away very impressed with the courage, determination, and ingenuity of the Israelis. In fact, after viewing a massive tree-planting effort to reclaim the desert in Israel, which has a climate akin to San Diego's, I launched a similar effort in Mission Trails Regional Park. That continues today as Mission Trails Regional Park Arbor Day.

Despite the relatively low pay and the demands on my time, I've never regretted my decision. Overall, being on the city council was a great experience. Some of my former colleagues at Luce, Forward did exceptionally well financially, but I haven't really spent much time looking back.

While on the council I did sometimes think about running for mayor, though I didn't intend to challenge Hedgecock. And I may even have had an occasional thought about being in Congress someday. But Jan hoped that one council term would get the political bug out of my system. And after the previous tumultuous two years, I too was leaning in that direction.

So I applied for and was appointed by Governor George Deukmejian as a municipal court judge. That was taking a chance but one that worked out well. It allowed me to combine my interest and training in the law and my penchant for public service as well as satisfying the long-term financial security that my growing family required. I was appointed in June 1985 and sworn in on July 1, leaving the council five months before the end of my first full term.

Looking back, maybe I should have run for re-election to the council and run for mayor when Roger Hedgecock was forced from office. If I'd lost, I still could have applied for a judgeship because Deukmejian, a Republican, remained governor until 1990. And if I'd won the mayor's seat, I could have applied for a judgeship when Pete Wilson was governor in the 1990s. However, given what I knew at the time, the judgeship was clearly the best choice.

But I have few (if any) misgivings about those years in the early 1980s. I loved the policy-wonk side of government—delving into complex issues, wrestling with budgets, building public facilities, and the like. The hardball confrontation politics was another matter. I could tolerate it during a campaign because then it had a beginning, a middle, and an end. But dealing with such conflict on an ongoing basis was uncomfortable at best and loathsome at worst. Four and a half years of that was enough for me.

Speaking at the San Diego Trolley East Line ground-breaking as MTDB chair (1985) (Credit: The San Diego Union-Tribune/ZUMAPRESS.com)

6

CREATING LEGACIES:
Mission Trails Park
and the San Diego Trolley

*"This then is the true joy in life, the being used
for a purpose recognized by yourself as a mighty one."*
—George Bernard Shaw

DURING MY YEARS ON THE San Diego City Council, I was probably best known as one of the founders of Mission Trails Regional Park (MTRP). The park's major landmarks include Cowles Mountain, the highest peak in the city at 1,592 feet; Lake Murray, a 200-acre water reservoir; and Mission Gorge, a scenic stretch of the San Diego River that contains remnants of the historic Old Mission Dam. At more than 6,000 acres, MTRP now is one of the largest urban parks in America. But in the late seventies and early eighties, it was still an evolving concept.

I'd long been interested in creating MTRP. For one thing, we lived just a mile or so from Mission Gorge. Further, the area reminded me of the forest preserves in the suburban Chicago area where I grew up, though with far fewer trees.

Plus, we would from time to time visit the Old Mission Dam site, also known as Padre Dam. It's a lovely spot, replete with history. The dam was built about 200 years ago by the Kumeyaay Indians under the direction of missionaries at Mission San Diego de Alcala, and its ancient remains still hold back a pleasant pool of water. But when I got on the Park & Rec Board, the dam site was the only City-owned portion of what would become the Mission Gorge area of the park.

By the time I joined the city council in December 1980, I had already been involved for several years in the early efforts to create the park as a member of the MTRP Citizens Advisory Committee, along with community leaders Dorothy Leonard and Mike Pent. As the new 7th District councilmember, I was appointed chair of the MTRP Task Force, composed of the region's elected officials charged with overseeing creation of the park. My new position gave me a leadership role at a critical stage in the park's development.

Threats to MTRP

During my tenure as MTRP Task Force chair, the park faced three big threats. The first one was a proposed housing project (Mission Dam Views), which would overlook the dam site. Complicating the matter was that this land actually was in the neighboring city of Santee. Clearly, the housing project, if built, would have disrupted the historical ambience. My guess is that the Santee City Council would have approved the project if I and others hadn't stepped in, got the San Diego City Council to buy the site, and later annex the property.

A second issue was the Navy's plan to build 1,500 units of military housing on federal land within the proposed park's boundaries. Because the Department of Defense already owned the property, it didn't need City approval. Though this development wouldn't have been as disruptive as the Santee proposal, it wouldn't have helped. Further, building the Navy housing was against the wishes of the Tierrasanta neighborhood, which preferred to be next to a park instead of military housing.

So the task was to persuade the Navy that it was not in its best interests to build there. With help from the San Diego Association of

Governments (SANDAG), I created a Military Housing Task Force to locate alternative sites for military family housing. The task force gave the Navy a viable alternative—that is, build clusters of housing in various parts of the city rather than one huge complex on the proposed parkland. This, we argued, would provide a better housing experience for its military families. What's more, we identified a number of locations.

Ultimately, the Navy abandoned its plans to build housing in MTRP and embraced the concept of dispersed housing clusters. For my efforts, I was awarded the Silver Seabee, the Navy Seabee's highest civilian award, and the first ever given to a civilian in the San Diego area.

The third threat came in the form of a 200-foot radio-TV antenna proposed for the top of Cowles Mountain. That would have destroyed not only the view *from* the peak, which is a popular hiking destination, but also the view *of* the peak from the main part of the park. Local TV and radio stations lobbied hard for the project, and the County of San Diego, which co-owned the peak with the City, also favored the project because it would collect rental fees. But our trump card was that the County couldn't proceed without the City's approval.

We were able to show the city council that allowing the project would be a bad policy decision because it would desecrate the highest point in the city. What's more, it would be a bad political decision because it would alienate District 7 voters forever. (At that time we had elections in which council aspirants were nominated by their districts but had to run citywide in a runoff. So every district got a say in who represented other areas of the city.) As a result, we were able to convince the San Diego City Council to vote down the antenna plan after a tough battle.

Expanding MTRP

At the same time we were fighting off assaults on the proposed park, we were also making steady progress in expanding its footprint. Between 1981 and 1984, the City of San Diego purchased almost 1,000 acres of open space lands in the Mission Gorge area, completing the critical land acquisitions that protected the San Diego River Gorge for posterity. And in 1985, we adopted the first MTRP Master Plan, which finalized park boundaries and remained the blueprint for park development for more than two decades.

The key to successfully acquiring MTRP land was working with City staff to devise criteria for the spending of the $65 million in open-space bond funds the voters had approved in 1978. Emphasizing large parcels and riparian habitat had the effect of moving MTRP up to the No. 2 spot on the list of potential acquisitions after Los Penasquitos Canyon. While it took some extra effort to push through the purchase of the Santee land, it helped that MTRP already was high on that priority list.

My most valuable ally on open-space issues was the City staff, particularly Nancy Acevedo, the acquisition coordinator. And the District 7 community was very supportive. However, some businesses and developers would have preferred MTRP land be used for private purposes, and some councilmembers were concerned that too much open-space bond money was being spent in my district. But we eventually, prevailed.

Reopening Lake Murray

While the Mission Gorge land acquisitions and the master plan adoption were essential to the creation of MTRP, my most visible and toughest battle was to reopen Lake Murray to the public. The lake had been closed and quarantined in 1977 due to an infestation of the water weed hydrilla. It had been fenced off for several years; residents weren't even allowed to walk near the lake, let alone get into the water.

The accepted treatment was to use chemical defoliants to retard the growth of the weed. But that was fairly ineffective because it had no impact on the roots. In fact at one point, the hydrilla got so thick that ducks could actually walk on the lake's surface. The only known way to

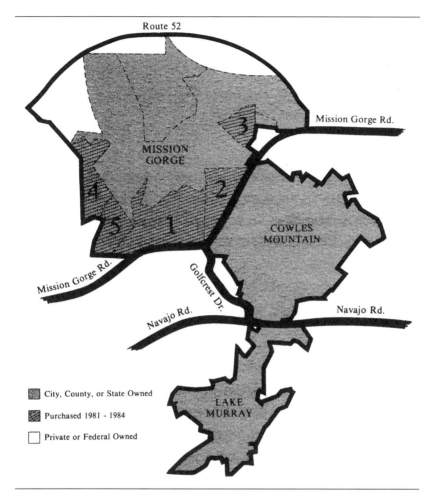

Route 52

Mission Gorge Rd.

MISSION GORGE

COWLES MOUNTAIN

Mission Gorge Rd.

Golfcrest Dr.

Navajo Rd.

Navajo Rd.

City, County, or State Owned

Purchased 1981 - 1984

Private or Federal Owned

LAKE MURRAY

Mission Trails Regional Park map

fix the situation was to drain the lake and remove all the sediment where the roots could otherwise thrive.

My early efforts to fight the hydrilla infestation met with stiff resistance in the City's water department, the County's agriculture department, and the State's fish and game commission, all of whom said hydrilla could not be eradicated. The City staff apparently liked Lake Murray being quarantined because that ensured residents couldn't use the lake and thus couldn't contaminate the reservoir's drinking water. State officials feared that the hydrilla would spread to other lakes and harm aquatic life, so they too supported the quarantine. And the County agriculture department appeared to resent an upstart politician from the city council telling it how to do its job.

So all three agencies stonewalled the effort. They had no real plan to solve the problem and reopen the lake. They needed a wake-up call.

Refusing to back down, I called for a probe of the leadership in the City's water department, demanding an independent audit of their management practices. A number of irregularities were uncovered. Shortly thereafter, the leadership in both the City water department and the County agriculture department was replaced with more creative managers, who found both the ways and the means to fight hydrilla.

I figured if we could put a man on the moon, we ought to be able get rid of a water weed. Sure enough, that was true. The new City water department management, led by Deputy Director Will Sniffin, devised a method using divers to suction out the hydrilla's roots from the lake bottom.

Bingo! Within two years, the hydrilla was gone—and apparently still is gone today. And with the help of Kathleen Thuner, the County's new agriculture director, we were able to convince the State fish and game people to lift the quarantine and reopen Lake Murray for public use.

The lake shore was officially reopened to the public on Memorial Day 1985. This was the first successful eradication of hydrilla from a water body in California, earning San Diegans the nickname "Hydrilla busters."

Chairing MTDB

In January 1983, Mayor Pete Wilson appointed me as one of the City of San Diego's representatives to the Metropolitan Transit Development Board (MTDB), the State-created agency that built and operated the

San Diego Trolley light-rail system. By 1983, the South Line, which runs from downtown San Diego to the Mexican border, had been successfully operating for more than a year. But the leaders of that initial effort were moving on, Mayor Pete Wilson to the U.S. Senate and former City Councilmember Maureen O'Connor to a campaign for mayor.

In September 1983, Maureen O'Connor resigned from MTDB after her unsuccessful mayoral bid, and I was elected the new chair. I wanted the job because I'd long been a fan of fixed-rail transit, having made frequent use of the "Elevated" system while living in the Chicago area. I particularly enjoyed the fact these electric systems didn't spew diesel fumes, as buses did, and ran on dedicated right-of-way so you could count on a smooth ride and timely arrivals. With its growing population, San Diego needed such a system.

I had had little to do with implementing the first leg (the South Blue Line) of the Trolley. But I definitely wanted to expand from that base. Wishing to set goals for a new generation of MTDB leaders, I gave the very first "State of the Trolley" address in January 1984. In my 1984 and 1985 addresses, I outlined five goals for San Diego's Metropolitan Transit System:

- Secure East Orange Line funding and begin construction
- Select a Bayside Line alignment and secure funding
- Identify a proposed North Mid-Coast Line alignment
- Determine a proposed Mission Valley Green Line alignment
- Consolidate San Diego's trolley and bus systems

By far the most significant of the five was securing funding for the proposed East Line to run from downtown San Diego through southeastern San Diego to the suburbs of La Mesa, Lemon Grove, and El Cajon. MTDB already owned the former San Diego and Arizona Eastern Railroad right-of-way that passed through those communities.

Funding the East Line

MTDB had been stymied for years in its quest to obtain funding for the East Line. The South Line had been built exclusively with California State funds obtained by State Senator Jim Mills. However, the State refused to provide any significant additional funding for the Trolley unless the federal government provided matching funds. But the Reagan administration had frozen funding for any "new-start" transit projects—that is, transit projects that had not previously received federal funds.

So in the spring of 1985 MTDB General Manager Tom Larwin and I flew to Washington, D.C., to renew MTDB's plea for federal funding for the East Line. We were warned that the House Appropriations Transportation Subcommittee had previously turned down San Diego's request.

But this year something was different: I'd been a classmate and friend of the son of House Transportation Subcommittee Chair Bill Lehman Sr. Bill Jr. and I had hung out together while attending Harvard Business School, including going on a ski trip in Vermont. I'd had very little contact with him since that time, but nonetheless I contacted Bill Jr. before going to Washington in hopes he might influence his dad.

As the House subcommittee chair called us to testify, Lehman senior looked at me sternly and said, "You must be my son Billy's friend from Harvard Business School." That silenced the hubbub in the committee room. Subcommittee staff hung up their phones. House subcommittee members paid attention to what we said. At the end of our presentation, Bill Lehman senior invited Tom and me to stop by his office at the end of the day, when we all got on a speaker phone to talk with his son Billy in Florida.

Several weeks later the House Appropriations Transportation bill was released and funding for the San Diego Trolley had been included. In all fairness, I was only part of a team effort. Senator Pete Wilson's intervention in the U.S. Senate and Mayor Roger Hedgecock's advocacy with the State Transportation Commission were equally important. And

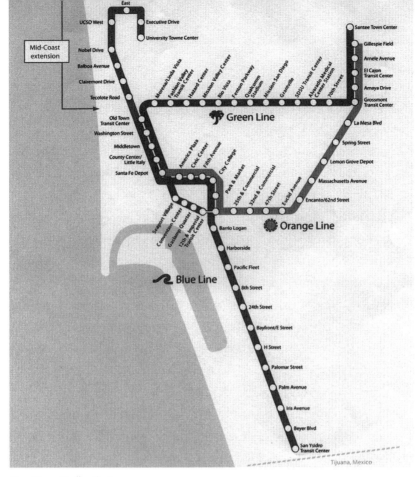

San Diego Trolley System map

MTDB staff provided the data and analysis necessary to "sell" the East Line project to federal and state agencies. But there was an important lesson from this experience: You never know when someone you befriend in your youth will reappear later in life when needed.

Building a Metropolitan Transit System

The breakthrough on federal funding for the East Line meant MTDB could develop a master plan for further extensions of the San Diego Trolley. We proceeded to adopt an alignment for the Bayside Line to loop around downtown from the Santa Fe Depot to the new convention center; we also convinced the San Diego Unified Port District to help pay for it. We approved a railway alignment for a North Line to run from the Santa Fe Depot to Old Town and eventually on to University of California, San Diego. And we adopted an alignment for a Mission Valley line to go from Old Town to Jack Murphy Stadium (now known as Qualcomm Stadium) and on to San Diego State University. That took care of the first four goals I had presented in my trolley addresses.

The fifth goal (consolidating the bus and trolley systems) had a bit more opposition because Senator Mills feared that a merger of the two systems could take our focus away from fixed-rail. The Trolley was financially successful, with an almost-unheard of 80 percent fare-box recovery. The bus system, though, was struggling. I too was concerned that the bus system's finances would hurt the trolley system. But the MTDB staff and council member Ed Struiskma convinced me that the merger would make both systems more cost effective and efficient. And I thought we might get a lot of bus-riding San Diegans to also take the Trolley.

In 1983 a study completed by the consulting firm Booz, Allen, & Hamilton recommended consolidating the operations of the San Diego trolley system with the San Diego bus system. Thus, even though I initially had reservations about consolidation, I eventually supported it as a means to provide more efficient mass-transit services to the region. On July 1, 2005, MTDB formally acquired San Diego Transit. It would be my last day as MTDB chair.

Looking back, I think the merger was the right decision. The Trolley has been a success, though it has expanded more slowly than I'd hoped. The East Line was opened in the 1980s. The Bayside Line began operating in the 1990s. The Mission Valley Line was finally completed in 2005. And the North Line should be finished sometime during the next decade.

So this period of the early 1980s was an important one for me. I got a lot done for District 7—such as the Jackson Drive extension, the Tierrasanta Library, the permit-parking district for the SDSU area, reopening Lake Murray, and, of course, helping protect and expand

Mission Trails Regional Park. And on the broader canvas of San Diego, I'm proud of having had a role in the Horton Plaza Shopping Center, the downtown convention center, the Trolley's East Line, and various open-space purchases, such as Los Penasquitos Canyon.

I had no regrets about having left Luce, Forward, though I'd enjoyed working there. The time demands of the council service were similar to those of practicing law. But the work itself was easier and more fun and gave me greater work schedule flexibility. And I believe my legal background was helpful in understanding municipal law and the lawsuits against the City.

I wanted my family to share in and enjoy some of these political experiences, and I believe they did. In addition to riding in parades and attending many "rubber chicken dinners," Jan, as mentioned earlier, was kissed by Tom Selleck at a volleyball match. Daughter Shannon served on the first children's advisory board of the new children's museum. Daughter Kelly got to give the key to the city to Donald Duck. And son Brian was able to mingle with players in the San Diego Padres dugout.

What I'd learned about myself during this period was that I really liked government policy and enjoyed making projects happen. But I was less enamored of hardball politics. And I still sought a bit more financial security. Those considerations drove my next move.

Superior Court Judge (1989–2000)

THE SAN DIEGO
SUPERIOR COURT:
Judging San Diego

"What does the Lord require of you but to do justice,
to love kindness, and to walk humbly with your God."
—*Micah 6:8*

BOTH THE CITY COUNCIL INFIGHTING and its low pay weighed on me. So getting back into the law held a lot of appeal. Sometimes the grass really is greener on the other side. After having given up a corporate job in order to go to law school, I had expected eventually to return to the legal world. I now saw a judgeship as the best path to meet my continuing long-term objectives: to make a meaningful contribution to society, have a degree of financial security, and still have time for my family.

I was not concerned about being re-elected to the council. In fact, by June 1985 I was unopposed in the September 1985 primary. But as previously mentioned, I applied for an appointment to the San Diego Municipal Court, rather than run again as District 7 councilmember. Gov. George Deukmejian appointed me to the bench in June 1985. In addition to my gratitude to the governor, I also owe a special debt of thanks to Judge Pete Riddle, who served on the governor's Judicial

Selection Committee and Congressman Clair Burgener, who championed my appointment.

San Diego Municipal Court

In those days, the muni courts were lower-level trial courts. That was where criminal arraignments, misdemeanor criminal trials, preliminary hearings in felony criminal cases, and minor civil trials were heard. (Later, in the 1990s, the Legislature consolidated the San Diego Municipal Court with the San Diego Superior Court.)

Because the muni court then handled primarily criminal matters, and I had no criminal trial experience, I had to work long hours initially to be a successful judge. After the first year, however, I began to feel pretty confident.

Though I enjoyed being a muni court judge, my four years on the court were not particularly remarkable. I served six months doing criminal arraignments and two and a half years presiding over preliminary hearings and misdemeanor criminal jury trials in the old downtown San Diego courthouse. During that time, I presided over hundreds of felony preliminary hearings and almost a hundred misdemeanor jury trials, mostly cases involving driving under the influence, petty theft, or domestic violence battery.

During my last year on the Municipal Court, I was supervising judge of the San Diego Municipal Court Civil Division. In that position, I heard the civil law and motion calendar, assigned civil cases for trial to other judges, and held hundreds of settlement conferences.

Again, I was comfortable there, though I did miss working on the big, community-shaping issues I'd been involved with as a councilmember. Yet I knew the muni court judgeship was a much better long-term opportunity. However, after four years, I was being urged by my colleagues—and in fact, felt obligated—to apply for the Superior Court.

*My children help me don judge's robe at judicial swearing-in ceremony
as wife Jan and Councilmembers Mitchell, Jones, and Struiksma look on (1985)*
(Credit: The San Diego Union-Tribune/ZUMAPRESS.com)

San Diego Superior Court

In July 1989 Gov. Deukmejian elevated me to the Superior Court. The Superior Court then was the trial court with jurisdiction over felony criminal trials, major civil trials, family court, juvenile court, and probate court. I was confident I could handle the Superior Court cases both legally and intellectually. But I was also very aware that it was a serious responsibility to preside over felony criminal cases, multimillion-dollar lawsuits, divorce and child-custody disputes, juvenile criminal and child-dependency proceedings, and the probate of wills, trusts, and estates. These are life-changing situations for the people who appear before the judge in these cases. What's more, I also felt a great duty to justify the public's confidence in the judiciary as one of the last bastions of integrity and fairness.

One of my strongest attributes as a judge was my willingness to do whatever research was necessary to make a correct decision. So in this situation, being something of a perfectionist was a positive trait. And I'm proud of the fact that I never had a criminal conviction reversed, though I did have a few sentences modified.

As a city council member, I was one of nine people engaged in decision making. In contrast, as a Superior Court judge, the decisions were often mine alone. And though my rulings usually impacted just the parties in a particular case—and not the community as a whole—it was sometimes a daunting task to referee these disputes and strive to make the correct decisions.

My first assignment was to hear felony criminal cases in the city of Vista in north San Diego County. As the newest Superior Court judge, I was assigned a courtroom in a trailer near the Vista courthouse. To say the least, the facilities were Spartan. For instance, when jurors were waiting outside the front door of the courtroom (and needed to be shielded from the accused at this stage), the defendants were brought from the jail in handcuffs via the back door of the trailer through my judge's chambers. That was a bit awkward, but because I was the most junior member of the court, I didn't complain.

Two of the first cases assigned to me in Vista were homicide cases. In one, *People v. Alberta Rader,* the defendant had killed her husband by shooting him in the head while he slept in bed after he had allegedly physically abused her.

The accused produced evidence showing scratches on her body. However, the prosecution argued she made the scratches herself because her husband had threatened to throw her out of the house and divorce her. But she claimed she feared for her life and acted only in self-defense.

After two and a half days of deliberation, the jury acquitted Alberta Rader. That was one of the first cases in San Diego in which a jury found a defendant not guilty by reason of self-defense in a domestic violence homicide.

The Hotel San Diego

After a year in Vista, I was reassigned to hear felony criminal cases in downtown San Diego. However, due to a shortage of courthouse facilities and my low seniority, I—along with five or six other judges—was assigned to the temporary courtrooms in the old Hotel San Diego. Needless to say, hotel guests often were surprised to see criminal defendants in handcuffs being escorted by County marshals through the hotel lobby on their way to court.

In other ways, too, the setup was odd, perhaps even comical if not for the gravity of the cases. For instance, the courtroom was in what had been a small hotel conference room. The cramped, odd-shaped room meant that some jurors could not see the defendant seated at the defense table. The judge's bench was elevated just a foot off the floor and right next to the witness stand; this made it possible for a seated witness to see if the judge was making notes. (One judge who had scribbled a note to himself, "The witness is lying," was corrected by the witness: "No, your honor, I'm *not*.")

This setup made the courtroom action seem less than serious at times. But while the arrangement wasn't great for instilling public confidence in the judicial process, we made it work. Opening into the conference room/courtroom were my chambers, which included a small bathroom. Because it was a hotel, I got fresh soap and towels each day.

Initially, I was supposed to be assigned civil cases and criminal cases in which the defendant was out on bail. But that plan was soon abandoned, and I began to be assigned homicide and sexual assault trials. Despite these difficult challenges, I was glad to be downtown again, at the heart of community affairs.

The most notable case I heard in the Hotel San Diego courtroom was *People v. Timothy Pemberton,* a homicide dubbed by the media as the "Good Samaritan Murder Trial." The defendant, a 22-year-old transient high on methamphetamine, had been burglarizing a woman's condo when she surprised him by returning home. As he fled, Gary Smith, who was laying carpet next door, chased the defendant two blocks, knocked him to the ground, and sought to wrest the gun from the burglar.

The defense argued that the gun went off in the struggle, killing the carpet layer. But witnesses said Pemberton pumped three bullets into the 35-year-old "good Samaritan" as Smith pleaded for his life.

After two days of deliberation, the jury found the defendant guilty of first-degree murder and other charges. I sentenced him to life in prison without the possibility of parole, noting that "in an era where we are short of heroes, Gary Smith was a legitimate hero."

The Downtown Courthouse

After a year of hearing cases in the old hotel, I was finally assigned to a real courtroom in the downtown San Diego Courthouse. During the decade of the 1990s, I presided over at least 250 felony criminal trials, including more than two dozen homicide cases. In addition I heard some 50 civil trials, such as wrongful death, medical malpractice, and property and contract disputes.

My case that received the most intense media attention was *People v. Robert Mack,* which was one of San Diego's first workplace-violence cases. Mack had been fired from his job at the General Dynamics Convair Division plant near the Lindbergh Field airport. After a grievance hearing to contest his termination, he shot and wounded his supervisor and killed a labor-relations manager.

Mack's defense was that he hadn't intended to murder anyone but instead took the gun to the plant to commit suicide, hoping to prompt investigations into what he felt was his unfair treatment after 24 years of service. But then he "blacked out" and remembered nothing about the murders.

The first trial ended in a hung jury. All jurors found the defendant guilty, but some found him guilty of first-degree murder, others second-degree murder, and a few voluntary manslaughter. Just minutes before his retrial was to begin, Mack changed his plea to guilty to second-degree

San Diego Superior Count Bench (1998)

murder. Under a plea bargain, he was sentenced to two consecutive life terms, the maximum allowed by law.

My most legally significant case was *People v. Melvin Burks.* The defendant, a 39-year-old parolee, was convicted of kidnapping and raping two women. One victim was an 84-year-old Sunday school teacher accosted in front of her church.

This was one of the earliest San Diego cases in which DNA evidence—then a relatively new and unproven technology—was admitted to identify the accused as the perpetrator. I spent several days reading and learning about DNA evidence before I ruled that it could be admitted in this case.

After a three-week trial, the jury deliberated for little more than a day before finding Burks guilty of all 11 charges brought against him. With a record of sex crimes dating back many years, he was sentenced to three consecutive life terms plus 56 years.

Many of the cases I heard were tragic and heartrending for the victims. One defendant was convicted of molesting nine young Scripps Ranch girls and sentenced to 50 years in prison. Another was convicted of raping and sexually assaulting four University City women and sentenced to 100 years. A third, accused of beating his pregnant girlfriend and killing the couple's eight-month-old fetus, was convicted of second-degree murder and sent to state prison for 20 years to life.

Life As a Judge

Being a judge was a lot different than being a councilmember. In judicial decision-making, maybe 99 percent of the time there is a legally correct ruling, a right answer, and your job as a judge is to find it. By contrast, political decision-making has no inherent right or wrong. You're confronted with a range of options, and then try to determine the best policy decision.

The toughest facet of being a judge is learning to let go. Sometimes you hear as many as 50 trials a year. Every week you need to be ready for a new case with new facts and new attorneys—and have the ability to not dwell on past ones. After analyzing the new facts and the law, you make the best decision you can—and, ideally, you move on. Second-guessing yourself is seldom helpful. As Judge Turrentine used to say, "If I make a mistake, the appellate court will tell me." That was one of the most helpful teachings from Judge T when I clerked for him.

The best part about being a judge is that you're in control of the courtroom. It's a small universe—you, the clerk, the court reporter, and the bailiff. And I had some terrific courtroom staff members over the years—particularly Carol Bonavolent (court clerk), Rilla Spousta (court reporter), and Glen Tremble (deputy marshal). You make all the decisions and pretty much at the pace you desire. And unlike a practicing attorney, you have the time to analyze the law thoroughly without worrying about filing deadlines or how you're going to justify the number of hours billed to the client.

One of the worst parts of a judge's job is the psychological toll the criminal calendar can take on you. Criminal courts are often sad places where day in and day out you see victims whose lives have been shattered, as well as the parents or partners of the defendants whose hearts have also been broken. You can end up feeling sorry for a lot of people.

Another downside is that it's a rather isolated existence. As a judge, you can't discuss pending cases with anyone (even your spouse) except fellow jurists. And you must keep your distance from lawyers who might someday appear in your court and, to a large degree, remain distant from the public as well. For a gregarious person like me who'd spent years meeting people, shaking hands, and immersing myself in community issues, that's a burden. But it's also an important boundary that has to be honored.

I always thought of being a judge as a way to perform public service without the abuse that elected officials get and without the enormous time demands that running for political office entails. Being a judge may have been the best job I've ever had—a rare combination of doing something that's always engrossing and at the same time is a worthwhile public service.

Outside Activities

Much of my off-duty life while on the bench, of course, revolved around my family. I taught all three kids to drive, helped each of them visit and apply to colleges, and spent hundreds of hours attending tennis matches, soccer games, and softball contests. In one particularly memorable bout of parental involvement, I took on the task of helping daughter Kelly become a softball pitcher. I stressed the importance of a routine and decreed she should throw at least 100 practice pitches a week. To her credit, she did. I know this because I was her catcher—50 weeks a year for 10 years. I caught somewhere between 50,000 to 100,000 pitches. Kelly went on to pitch four years on the high school varsity softball team and be named to the all-county first team twice. From that experience, Kelly learned that with enough dedication, one can be successful.

I also kept active in judicial affairs beyond the walls of my courtroom. From 1991 through 1998, I was a member of Governor Pete Wilson's San Diego County Judicial Selection Committee, which recommended potential judges to the governor. My long-time friendship with Pete allowed me to have a say in the selection of dozens of judges for appointment. For several years, I was also an elected member of the San Diego Superior Court Executive Committee. In that capacity I spent an entire weekend with fellow Superior Court Judge Dick Haden poring through books of quotations and legal references. Our mission? To come up with 18 famous statements that were to be etched on the walls of the new Hall of Justice. (Sample: "Injustice anywhere is a threat to justice everywhere," The Rev. Martin Luther King Jr.)

The California Superior Court is the battlefield of contemporary society where disputes are settled. And my judicial colleagues, such as Mike Bollman, Dick Haden, Terry Knoepp, and Chuck Wickersham and many others, were intelligent, dedicated, and collegial public servants with whom I was proud to serve. And the attorneys who appeared before us almost always were hard working and dedicated to their clients' interests. In fact, I came to believe that lay people often misjudge lawyers because they don't appreciate the challenges attorneys face. Being a practicing lawyer has become more difficult as attorneys struggle to meet the court's demands and those of their clients. I particularly admired those in the offices of the district attorney, public defender, and other government entities who tend to see themselves performing a public service, as opposed to being motivated by money.

In many ways, being a judge better suited my personality and work habits than did politics. So while I may have been a better judge than a politician, I missed being involved in community issues. After 14 years on the bench, I kept hearing the call to return to politics as a way to make a bigger contribution to society. As I joked to one journalist who inquired about my zigzag career path, "Either I'm a Renaissance man . . . or I can't decide what I'm going to do when I grow up."

Murphy family, election night, November 2000—Kelly, Brian, Dick, Jan, Shannon

8

THE 2000 MAYORAL ELECTION:
An Upset Victory

"Chance favors the prepared mind."
—*Louis Pasteur*

THE LURE OF LAW, on the one hand, and of politics on the other tugged me during the 1990s, creating mixed emotions. I liked being a judge and thought the job was a good match for my skills, personality, and education. But I still harbored an urge to make a larger contribution to society, and politics was probably a better place to do that. So I considered running for Congress in both 1992 and 1994. However, I was reluctant to give up my judgeship at that point because I had a child in college, another in high school, and a third in junior high. So leaving the bench to take a gamble on that Congressional seat didn't seem prudent.

The Decision to Run

But by 1999, the idea of running for mayor of San Diego had increasing appeal. Why? Well, for one thing, a lot of the big issues the City was grappling with—such as the effort to build a downtown ballpark—were enmeshed in lawsuits and ethical issues for which my legal background might be an advantage. Second, I had an MBA and business experience and could understand financial issues. What's more, I'd served on the city council so I understood city government and saw myself as a consensus-builder at a time when mayor-council relations were rocky. And perhaps most important, I'd thought a lot about the city's future and had a vision of protecting San Diego's vaunted quality of life. No one else who was presumed to be running seemed to have a similar vision.

I was concerned that the city was continuing to let its unique quality of life erode because of explosive growth and environmental degradation. In fact, I felt the city was at a turning point. Not only was it the start of the new millennium, but San Diego also was sliding toward becoming more akin to Los Angeles. Growth was out of control, traffic congestion was worsening, beaches were polluted, crime was increasing, and neighborhoods were deteriorating. It seemed to me that we were letting slip away the qualities that make San Diego such a special place. Something had to be done. That may have seemed like an odd stance for a Republican, but I've long been an environmental moderate and a fiscal conservative.

Taking all these factors into consideration, I felt a strong call—from God—to run. I owed that to myself and to the public. Still, that wasn't a decision to be made lightly. The good news was that I could take a leave of absence as a Superior Court judge, so I could return to the bench if I lost the election. The bad news was that it was an *unpaid* leave of absence, so I would be foregoing my judge's salary for at least a year. And I had to consider that my wife Jan had already put up with my quitting Bank of America to attend Stanford Law School in 1972 and then leaving Luce, Forward to accept an appointment to the San Diego City Council in 1980.

However, I was content to run and let the chips fall where they would. That attitude made the election a more pleasant experience compared to some others I've been involved in.

Jan was reluctantly supportive. She didn't want me to leave the bench, but felt she should support my quest if it was that important to me. She didn't want me to look back a decade later and regret not having run.

The Primary Election

From the beginning, the mayoral election of 2000 was supposed to be a two-person race between San Diego County Supervisor Ron Roberts and Centre City Development Corporation Chair Peter Q. Davis. Roberts had held political office for more than a decade and had a reputation as a prolific fundraiser. Davis was a wealthy retired banker prepared to spend more than a million dollars of his own money to get elected. There were also three well-respected San Diego City Councilmembers running: Barbara Warden, Byron Wear, and George Stevens. No one gave me much of a chance.

Once I decided to run, my first step was to assemble a good campaign team. I hired campaign consultant John Kern, my former city council chief of staff and good friend, to be campaign manager. Along with

San Diego 2000 mayoral candidates (left to right) Ron Roberts, Pete Davis, Barbara Warden, and Dick Murphy. (Photo by Mark Brenner/ Rancho Bernardo Sun)

John came his young and talented assistant, Paola Avila. Republican attorney Bill Baber joined us as campaign treasurer. And public relations consultant Kate Seiber assumed the responsibility for fundraising and press relations.

Our campaign slogan was "Leadership with 2020 Vision." The slogan succinctly articulated our campaign message that San Diego needed a mayor with a clear vision for what San Diego should be in the year 2020, along with the courage and competence to implement that vision. The vision was San Diego as America's safest city with freeways that weren't parking lots and neighborhoods to be proud of. The implied criticism of my opponents was that career politicians are nearsighted; they see only as far as the next election.

In the broadest sense, our platform was that the quality of life in San Diego should be better in 2020 than it was in 2000. More specifically, I articulated five goals, each with its own slogan:

- Reduce traffic congestion—"Freeways That Are Not Parking Lots"
- Make neighborhoods more attractive—"Neighborhoods to be Proud of"
- Eliminate Water Pollution Problems—"Clean up Our Beaches and Bays"
- Reduce Crime—"Make San Diego America's Safest City"
- Slow Growth—"Uncontrolled Growth Is Not Inevitable"

Pete Davis, the millionaire banker, with his knowledge of economic issues probably would have made a good mayor. Ron Roberts, though highly experienced, was too close to development interests, I thought. All the city councilmembers—Byron Wear, George Stevens, and Barbara Warden—were likeable, but not very electable. And no one had my vision of a better quality of life for San Diego, and how to implement it. Bottom line: I thought I was the best qualified but not the most electable.

With a field of six viable candidates (and six additional "minor" ones), we figured that if I could capture at least 15 percent of the vote in the March primary, I'd have a shot at qualifying for the runoff election in November. If no one captured 50 percent of the vote in the March primary, the top two vote-getters would compete in the November general election. A big question, though: Could I extend my support beyond my former city council district?

We targeted three large voter groups — Republicans, military veterans, and residents of my former city council district. Early endorsements from former Republican U.S. Congressman Clair Burgener and incumbent 7th District Councilmember Judy McCarty gave us credibility with these groups.

The *Veterans Journal* monthly newspaper, headed by David Brown, promoted my candidacy within the veterans' community. In it the newspaper endorsed my veterans affairs plan for the city:

- Financing 50 percent of the cost of the Veterans Day Parade
- Creating a full-time military and veterans' affairs liaison in the Mayor's office
- Building a veterans' memorial garden in Balboa Park
- Constructing a new veterans' cemetery in San Diego County
- Supporting Operation Stand Down and a winter shelter for homeless veterans

We also targeted smaller groups with whom I had a unique relationship—University of Illinois, Harvard Business School, and Stanford Law School alums, Alpha Tau Omega fraternity brothers, San Carlos Methodist Church congregants, and even Proviso West High School grads in San Diego.

We devoted almost all of our efforts for the first three months to political fundraising. This was a lot harder in the primary because few people were expecting me to run, or to win. So I had to call old friends and ask for the then-maximum $250 contribution. Even my wife's siblings, Phyllis, Preston, and Beverly, contributed. That took great discipline; I had a goal of getting 10 donors to agree each day. I did not enjoy that part.

In order to establish our campaign's viability, we had a single goal of raising $100,000 by the first fundraising-reporting deadline of June 30, 1999. We focused on raising money from my many attorney friends as well as former political supporters from my city council days. On June

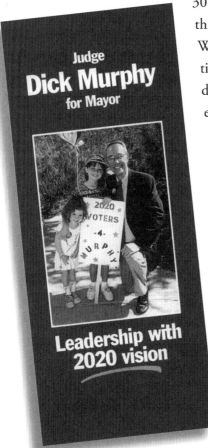

Judge
Dick Murphy
for Mayor

Leadership with
2020 vision

30, we reported raising $101,000, placing third in fundraising behind Roberts and Warden. I was buoyed by John Kern's assertion that "to triumph in an election, you don't need to raise the most money, just enough to win."

I believe if you know exactly what you're doing—that is, you have a plan— you can win. Many races just happen. The candidate doesn't have money, a vision, or a campaign strategy. So we sought to avoid all those mistakes and ended up having a campaign plan that envisioned spending $250,000, including buying TV time.

During the summer of 1999, we convinced my long-time friend and

Campaign brochure (2000)

community volunteer Rachel Shira to join the team as campaign coordinator to run our new campaign headquarters and organize a grassroots campaign. We focused on two projects. First, posting 1,000 campaign signs in people's front yards, an effort led by Pacific Southwest Airlines co-founder Leo Leonard. Second, mailing 25,000 postcards from supporters to their friends urging them to vote for me, a huge task directed by retired Qualcomm executive Tom Lancaster and other members of San Carlos United Methodist Church.

The fall of 1999 was a nonstop blur of candidate forums, fundraisers and friendraisers, and speeches to anyone who would listen. For example, as a San Diego Rotary Club 33 member, I was invited to speak at virtually all 25 Rotary clubs in the City of San Diego. By December 1999, a *San Diego Union-Tribune* poll showed 11 percent of the voters favoring Davis, 8 percent for Roberts, 6 percent for Stevens, 5 percent for Warden, 4 percent for Wear, 3 percent for me, and 57 percent undecided. The 57 percent undecided meant the election was still up for grabs.

By mid-January 2000, Davis had loaned his campaign $800,000. Roberts had raised more than $600,000. Warden had raised over $400,000. We had doubled our contributions but still had raised only $200,000. We posted our 1,000 yard signs in front yards across the city in January. We mailed 25,000 postcards from supporters to their friends in February. We had just enough money to run television ads during the last two weeks before the primary election on March 7.

A *San Diego Union-Tribune* poll conducted in mid-February showed Davis favored by 13 percent of the voters with Roberts at 10 percent, Warden at 8 percent, Stevens at 7 percent, Wear at 6 percent, and me at 5 percent. Sensing victory within her reach, Warden launched television ads attacking Davis for supporting tax increases and attacking Roberts for promoting growth. At the same time, we ran our two TV ads, one touting fiscal responsibility and one opposing traffic congestion and growth. The juxtaposition could not have been better.

When primary election night finally arrived on March 7, 2000, the pundits were still predicting a November runoff election between Davis and Roberts. As voting results began to pour in, Roberts was running first, Davis was placing second, and I was trailing a close third behind Davis. By the end of election night, Davis had just a 268-vote lead over me, out of more than 250,000 mayoral ballots cast.

As the absentee vote count dragged on for several days after the election, Davis's lead kept shrinking. Always liking an underdog who comes from behind to win, the public's attention became riveted on the drama of the close absentee-vote count. After the final votes were tabulated six days after the election, I had placed second in the primary election and beaten Davis by a mere 169 votes (not exactly a landslide victory).

We'd had a good strategy, good execution by our volunteers, good luck, and perhaps Divine intervention. Our three-pronged strategy had allowed us to focus our limited resources on wooing District 7 residents, Republicans, and veterans. Plus, we had been very disciplined financially. Another piece of good luck was that Warden's ads attacked Davis (for favoring higher taxes) and Roberts (for being in developers' pockets). In fact, Barbara may have made the difference for us.

The General Election

The euphoria of the come-from-behind upset victory quickly faded into the stark realization that we were the distinct underdog in the November 2000 general election. Roberts had received more than 25 percent of the vote in the primary; I had gotten approximately 15 percent. Roberts had raised more than $750,000 in campaign contributions in the primary; we had raised only $250,000. And Roberts had locked up endorsements from much of the "establishment." Basically, it appeared that it was Roberts' race to lose.

But I was pretty fatalistic about the endeavor. If God wanted me to win, I would. If not, I'd go back to being a judge and that would be OK.

I had nothing to lose except another eight months of salary. This was a very liberating attitude.

During the spring and early summer, the campaign was shaping up as a classic "geraniums vs. smokestacks" race. As a professional architect and longtime politician, Roberts was the darling of the developers—supported by the building industry, labor unions, and the business community. Although I was a conservative on issues such as taxes, crime, and national defense, I was an environmental moderate—alarmed that uncontrolled growth had congested our freeways, polluted our beaches, and destroyed our open space. Roberts and I pretty much agreed on fiscal issues but diverged on the environment.

Our big break was Roberts' decision to make ethics an issue in the campaign. In mid-August, he outlined his proposal for a city ethics commission, claiming long-time support for an ethics panel. Supporters of outgoing San Diego Mayor Susan Golding immediately pounced, calling us to point out that Roberts had opposed Golding's ethics commission proposal while Roberts was a member of the San Diego City Council during the 1990s. A few weeks later, on the Roger Hedgecock radio talk show, Roberts said he had voted for an ethics commission while on the city council, a statement he later admitted was incorrect.

By the end of August, I had outlined a much more detailed proposal for an ethics commission, one with power to issue subpoenas, conduct audits, and levy fines. It was virtually the same ethics commission proposal that Mayor Golding's Ethics Advisory Board had previously proposed and Roberts had opposed. The San Diego Union-Tribune headline read "Murphy One-Ups Rival with Ethics Panel Proposal," and that paper's editorial board endorsed my ethics proposal in early September.

The ethics issue had surfaced when it came to light that San Diego City Councilmember Valerie Stallings had voted to approve the San Diego Padres' new downtown ballpark after buying stock in an initial public offering of a Texas software company that was headed by San

Diego Padres' owner John Moores. After Roberts raised the ethics issue, I called for Stallings to resign and challenged Roberts to join me in calling for her resignation if he was serious about ethics in City government. Roberts, a longtime Stallings political ally, declined.

By September, a U.S. Attorney investigation into the dealings between Moores and Stallings was headline news. In mid-September, it came to light that Roberts had taken six flights on San Diego Padres' charter planes or the Padres owner's private jet. Roberts claimed he had reimbursed the Padres for the cost of all the flights. Sometime later, Roberts finally admitted that one flight had not been paid for. By mid-October, the *Los Angeles Times* summed up the mayoral campaign in a headline that read: "Integrity Trumps Other Issues in San Diego's Mayoral Race."

The Roberts campaign's handling of the ethics issue changed the dynamics of the race. On October 15, the *San Diego Union-Tribune* endorsed me for mayor, citing my independence from special interests. On October 16, the *San Diego Daily Transcript* endorsed my candidacy, deviating from its long-standing policy of not endorsing political candidates. On October 17, the Sierra Club endorsed me, stating I was the better choice to protect the quality of life in San Diego. And on October 28, seven Latino organizations announced their endorsement of my campaign.

The weekend before the election, a poll by local public broadcast station KPBS showed me leading Roberts 43 percent to 38 percent, with 19 percent of voters undecided. But a KGTV poll put Roberts ahead of me 46 percent to 44 percent. The race was a toss-up.

On election day, I prevailed with a 52 percent to 48 percent victory margin. Again it seemed that Divine providence had deemed that I should win the election.

Without the ethics issue, Roberts probably would have won. Which validates the view I expressed in an earlier chapter—most races are lost by the losers rather than won by the victors.

I wasn't exactly a fresh face (having been on the council before), but I was definitely an outsider who hadn't held political office for 15 years. My status was unique: I had city council experience but was not a career politician, and I had establishment-type credentials without really being supported by the establishment. In the year 2000, with ethics issues at the forefront and politicians generally disdained, that was a good position to be in. In truth and in retrospect, my "non-politician" label probably contributed more to my victory than the well-thought-out platform that I was so proud of.

My family had been wonderful during the long campaigns. While my daughters were away at college, son Brian attended campaign events and acted as sort of a special-campaign-advisor-on-appealing-to-younger-voters. My wife Jan went to every event and volunteered hundreds of hours in our campaign headquarters. Thus, in addition to working part-time as a pediatric physical therapist to support the family, she played a big role in helping me win—even though she wasn't sure she wanted me to win.

In fact, my goal from the beginning hadn't been to win as much as to run a good campaign. As it turned out, doing the latter accomplished the former.

What if I hadn't won? I would have gone back to the Superior Court and stayed there until retirement. It is unlikely I would have run for office again. And while I wouldn't have had any regrets, I'd probably have a better pension at this point.

The lesson from this experience is that in a political election, with no incumbent office holder, results can be unpredictable. Almost anyone can win with the right blend of money, message, strategy, and good luck. But events beyond your control can also determine your destiny.

Mayor of San Diego (2000–2005)

9

THE MAYORAL FIRST TERM:
The 10-Goal Vision

"Vision without action is a daydream.
Action without vision is a nightmare."
—Japanese proverb

WHEN THE EXCITEMENT OF WINNING the election died down, it was time to switch gears and move from campaign mode into the actual job of leading the city into the 21st century. All those campaign pledges, including my highest priority of creating a city ethics commission, meant little without a plan to turn them into reality. And as I prepared to go from the courthouse to the mayoral offices on the 11th floor of city hall, I was pondering the blueprint for my first term.

The move from one workplace to the other was only a few blocks' distance, but worlds apart in atmosphere. I was leaving the orderly, highly procedural, generally low-profile courtroom to step into a glaring city spotlight where debates on controversial issues could get downright rowdy and where perceptions—even distorted ones—could take on a life of their own.

The change from judge to mayor also was going to mean far less family time. I was glad that my children were busy with their own lives.

My son, Brian, was at the University of San Diego Law School. Daughter Shannon had graduated from UC Berkeley and was in grad school at UC Davis. My other daughter, Kelly, was an undergraduate at UCLA. My wife would have to share my time with scores of City officials and more than a million constituents. I tried to make up for that by bringing her to political functions or special events. We did have dinners with England's Prince Andrew, newscaster Diane Sawyer, and actor Harrison Ford, but many nights she was home alone while I worked.

As a former city councilmember and a long-time observer of the local political scene, I had no illusions when I became mayor. I would be perceived as the city's political leader. Still, under the weak-mayor system, I could cast only a single vote for any of my proposals. I needed at least four of my council colleagues to join me to pass anything with a simple majority. Having a positive relationship with the city council would be imperative.

Council consensus building was further complicated by district-only elections approved in 1988. Under this system, city council members are elected by voters in their districts in both the primary and runoff elections. So their issues often stopped at district boundaries. Earlier, when I had served on the city council, the primaries were held in the council districts, but the runoff elections were citywide. Back then, city council candidates, as well as the mayor, had to be responsive to issues affecting the entire city.

Given these challenges, the best way forward—perhaps the only truly effective way—was to forge partnerships on the city council and to gather support in the community at large. I wanted to avoid the fractious rivalries that had existed between prior mayors and councilmembers, which had impeded the City's progress.

The need for collaboration went beyond winning over individual councilmembers. I wanted as many San Diegans as possible to feel they had a stake in the future. The timing was right. At the start of the millennium, the civic mood was especially hopeful and optimistic. And the city council would have a fresh look. In the 2000 election, the electorate swept into office a new mayor and five other city council newcomers.

I spent the four weeks between the November 2000 election and the December 2000 inauguration hiring a strong mayoral office staff. John Kern, my campaign manager and chief of staff when I had previously served on the city council, agreed to stay on as chief of staff in the mayor's office. Other senior staff members eventually included Deputy Chief of Staff Paola Avila, Rules Committee Consultant Bill Baber, senior policy advisors Tom Story and Dennis Gibson, Press Secretary Colleen Rudy Windsor, schedule coordinators Rachel Shira and Cynthia Lewis, Community Outreach Director Bruce Williams, Chief of Protocol Elena Salsitz, Arts and Culture Liaison Gayle Hom, and Military and Veterans Liaison Rudy Fernandez.

With my staff in place, I was ready to introduce my mayoral priorities. At my inauguration on Dec. 4, 2000, I delivered an inaugural address entitled "New Partnerships, New Beginnings." I emphasized the fact that six of the nine members of the city council, myself included, were newly elected—an unprecedented changeover in San Diego history. I would try to forge a partnership and positive relationship with each councilmember.

I discussed our plan to give members of the public an opportunity to share opinions with my administration. To accomplish that, I created six advisory boards reflecting the diversity of the city:

- An Environmental Advisory Board chaired by Carolyn Chase, former chair of the San Diego chapter of the Sierra Club
- A Veterans Advisory Board, chaired by Col. Pete Houben, the United Veterans Council Veteran of the Year in 2000
- An African-American Advisory Board, chaired by William Jones, businessman and former San Diego city councilmember

- A Latino Advisory Board, chaired by Josie Calderon, president of the Mexican American Business and Professional Association
- An Asian-Pacific Islander Advisory Board, chaired by Mitsuo Tomita, a medical doctor who was a past chair of the Union of Pan-Asian Communities
- A Lesbian, Gay, Bisexual, and Transgender (LGBT) Advisory Board, chaired by Art Thompson, Executive Director of the Lesbian and Gay Men's Community Center

These mayoral advisory boards were more than symbolic. They drew good people from their communities into City government circles and added insight to our debates. They often recommended appointees to other city boards and commissions. In some cases, they had an important role in creating civic projects.

For instance, the Veterans Advisory Board worked with me to design and construct a veterans memorial garden in Balboa Park. As part of my campaign for mayor, I had promised the veteran community to pursue building this garden adjacent to the Veterans Memorial Center in Balboa

San Diego mayoral inauguration (2000) (Credit: The San Diego Union-Tribune/ZUMAPRESS.com)

Park. To fulfill that pledge, I had obtained City funds to develop a master plan for the site. However, the City did not have the money to actually construct the garden. But success rewards the prepared.

Fortuitously, Governor Gray Davis's Chief of Staff Lynn Schenk contacted me and City Councilmember Toni Atkins (who represented the Balboa Park area) to inquire if we had any recommendations for capital improvements in Balboa Park that the governor could fund with State park bonds. Jumping at the opportunity, we recommended among several projects construction of the Veterans Memorial Garden, which was particularly appropriate for Governor Davis, who is a fellow Army veteran. The Veterans Memorial Garden was formally dedicated in 2005.

My first State of the City speech in January 2001 was titled "A Vision for San Diego in the Year 2020: A City Worthy of Our Affection." While San Diegans were already fond of their city, I said, we needed to protect the city's quality of life if San Diego was going to remain worthy of that affection.

I then outlined 10 goals I wanted to accomplish during my years as mayor. These goals, if realized, would make San Diego a city worthy of our affection in the year 2020. They covered a wide gamut of civic activities. Two involved major brick-and-mortar projects—the downtown ballpark and a central library—that I inherited at critical junctures in their development. Others were planning or good-government goals that tend to rest lightly on public consciousness but are no less important to the well-being of the city. Together, these goals were intended to be my vision for San Diego and a standard by which my success or failure as its mayor could be measured.

GOAL #1:
Establish an Ethics Commission

When I ran for the mayor's office, an investigation was under way into allegations that City Councilmember Valerie Stallings had received gifts from San Diego Padres owner John Moores and failed to disclose them. Worse yet, she had continued to vote on matters related to the downtown ballpark, which would be the Padres' home. The investigation into this conflict of interest brought ballpark construction to a halt, a situation that ended in late January 2001 when Stallings resigned from the council and pled guilty to a misdemeanor.

I felt that the City's credibility had been tarnished by this and that better ethical oversight was a must. Since ethics had been a central issue in the mayoral campaign, I made establishing an ethics commission my top goal. I wanted a strong and impartial watchdog that would help restore the public's confidence in the City's leadership by doing the following:

- Developing a new City ethics code
- Investigating violations of the ethics code
- Imposing penalties for violations of the ethics code
- Providing training to City employees on ethics issue.
- Giving advice to City employees on ethics questions

During 2001, we created the City's first Ethics Commission. Working with City Attorney Casey Gwinn's staff and two members of Mayor Golding's Ethics Advisory Board, Dan Eaton and Dorothy Leonard, we drafted an ordinance to create a City Ethics Commission in early 2001. After a battle over the process of selecting ethics commissioners, the new city council adopted a modified version of my proposal in June. Under the compromise for choosing ethics commissioners, the council and city attorney would make the initial nominations, the mayor would choose from this list, which would then go back to the city council for confirmation.

In August 2001 I nominated and the council confirmed the first seven ethics commissioners for the City of San Diego: Lisa Foster, Albert

Gaynor, Charles La Bella, Dorothy Leonard, April Riel, Dorothy Smith, and Gregory Vega. In November the commission hired its first executive director, Charles Walker, former ethics officer for the FBI.

The following year, we empowered the Ethics Commission, and the process took off. This was accomplished by having the ethics commissioners draft a comprehensive ethics code for city officials, which the city council adopted. The council also approved the commission's proposal for investigative and administrative enforcement procedures, enabling the commission to deal with alleged violations.

For the first time, we had the tools to oversee and enforce ethics rules, both internally and for the City's electoral process. We could advise candidates and ballot measure committees and audit campaign committees. We also made ethics training mandatory for all City officials and began training classes.

By the end of 2002, goal No. 1 was essentially completed. In my opinion, the San Diego Ethics Commission has been an unqualified success and one of my best accomplishments as mayor.

GOAL #2:
Reduce Traffic Congestion

The Texas Transportation Institute had issued a report showing that San Diego had the eighth worst roadway congestion of any city in America. Following up on a campaign promise to have freeways that were not parking lots, I made reducing traffic congestion my second goal. This included three different strategies:

- Build more freeway capacity
- Expand mass transit
- Develop a smart growth land use strategy that would discourage urban sprawl and reduce auto trips

To address the need for more freeway capacity, I appointed myself to serve as the City's representative on the San Diego Association of Governments (SANDAG) board of directors, which controlled Transnet freeway construction funds. (Transnet is San Diego County's ½ cent sales tax dedicated to transportation improvements.) In addition, I partnered with a new councilmember, District 5's Brian Maienschein, to form the Freeway Congestion Strike Team. The heavily congested Interstate 15 corridor ran through Maienschein's district, so he was eager to join the cause of reducing traffic jams. The strike team worked on many freeway issues, among them measuring traffic congestion, building more managed lanes, and promoting carpooling. However, our primary achievement was to establish a unique partnership between the City, SANDAG, and the California Department of Transportation (CALTRANS) to accelerate the completion of State Route 56, which connects I5 and I15 at city's northern edge. Finished in 2004, the project was celebrated with a grand opening attended by thousands.

As an advocate for mass transit expansion, I also appointed myself to serve as one of the City's representatives on the Metropolitan Transit Development Board (MTDB). At the time, MTDB was responsible for developing and operating the San Diego trolley and bus system in metropolitan San Diego County. Our most significant accomplishment was beginning and completing construction of the San Diego Trolley Mission Valley Green Line from Qualcomm Stadium to San Diego State University and on to East San Diego County.

Finally, to implement a smart growth strategy, I worked with the City Planning Department led by Gail Goldberg to develop the City of Villages land use plan. It envisioned rebuilding San Diego's older neighborhoods as intimate, walkable villages. It would integrate higher density housing, office buildings, retail stores, schools, parks, and other public facilities into one neighborhood, thereby discouraging urban sprawl and reducing auto trips. Opponents argued that it would overdevelop some neighborhoods. But after several raucous public hearings, the plan was adopted by the city council in 2002 and won several awards for innovative land use planning.

GOAL #3:
Create Neighborhoods to Be Proud of

My belief is that for San Diego to be truly worthy of the public's affection, its citizens must live in attractive neighborhoods. When I took office in December 2000, the city had a multimillion-dollar backlog of needed improvements to deteriorated public infrastructure in its older neighborhoods. To help jump-start this effort, I teamed up with another city council newcomer, Toni Atkins, whose District 3 included many of the city's older areas in mid-city, to pursue my third goal, creating neighborhoods to be proud of. Part of that goal would be implementing the City of Villages plan. To that end, Toni and I organized the Smart Growth Implementation Committee, which selected five pilot village projects in older communities like Mid-City and San Ysidro. The City of Villages concept not only discouraged urban sprawl and reduced traffic congestion, it also was a way to promote the redevelopment of older neighborhoods and develop more affordable housing.

We were able to provide some of the city's older communities with new parks, libraries, fire stations, sidewalks, streetlights, and landscaped center medians. Working with Drew Potocki, the City's urban forester, we also launched the Community Forest Initiative, a plan to plant 100,000 new trees citywide by the year 2020. Not only do trees beautify neighborhoods, they reduce urban runoff, improve air quality, and decrease energy consumption by naturally cooling neighborhoods. By the end of 2004, the City had planted 12,770 trees throughout the city.

Our most significant accomplishment, however, was the implementation of a program to underground virtually every overhead utility line in the city by the year 2020. This involved protracted negotiations with the affected utility companies: San Diego Gas and Electric, Pacific Bell, Cox Communications, and Time Warner. An even bigger hurdle was gaining approval from the California Public Utilities Commission. Although the timetable proved to be overly optimistic, all San Diego neighborhoods will eventually benefit from the safety, reliability, and aesthetics of underground utility lines.

GOAL #4:
Clean Up Our Beaches and Bays

In the year before my election, San Diego's polluted beaches and bays were a major civic embarrassment. The city had 364 sewer spills and more than 2,300 beach postings and closures due to water pollution during the year 2000. To tackle this problem, I teamed up with the newly elected District 1 Councilmember Scott Peters, who represented coastal La Jolla,

SeaWorld's Shamu joins me in promoting phone book recycling (2001)

to work toward cleaning up our bays and beaches as my fourth goal. We created the Clean Water Task Force and set a target of reducing sewer spills and beach closures by 50 percent by the year 2004.

Working with the city's Metropolitan Wastewater Department, led by Scott Tulloch, we were able to reduce sewer spills by more than 50 percent by 2003, a year ahead of schedule, by doing the following:

- Tripling sewer line replacement and rehabilitation from 20 to 60 miles per year
- Inspecting with robotic cameras the interior of 1,000 miles of older sewer pipes
- Cleaning for the first time ever the entire 3,000-mile sewer system

Although reducing sewer spills had a significant impact on cleaning up our beaches and bays, the majority of San Diego's beach and bay water pollution was actually caused by contaminated urban runoff. So working with the city's Stormwater Pollution Prevention Division, led by Karen Henry, we also reduced beach postings and closures by more than 50 percent by 2003. This was accomplished by doing the following:

- Adopting an Urban Runoff Management Plan to reduce pollutants in stormwater runoff
- Securing millions of dollars of federal and state grants to build low-flow diversion projects that redirected contaminated runoff into the sewer system
- Implementing an Emmy Award-winning "Think Blue" publicity campaign to raise public awareness of how individual behavior can prevent polluted urban runoff

By any measure, our effort to clean up San Diego's beaches and bays was a big success. The city's frequent sewer spills and numerous beach closures due to pollution had been a significant issue in the late 1990s. By focusing on the issue and investing significant sums of money to address this problem, we quickly and dramatically solved the problem. By the 2004 election campaign, the issue was nearly forgotten.

Goal #5:
Form a San Diego Regional Airport Authority

The San Diego International Airport at Lindbergh Field began operation in 1928 along the north side of San Diego Bay. It has a single runway located on 661 acres, a postage stamp for an airport. Most studies show that the airport will reach capacity around the year 2020, inconveniencing local travelers, limiting economic growth, and diminishing air safety. All efforts to build a new San Diego Airport in the last 50 years have failed.

Part of the reason for that failure was that responsibility for the airport was shared by two different government entities. The San Diego Unified Port District operated the airport and garnered its revenues, which could be tapped for other port projects. The San Diego Association of Governments (SANDAG) was in charge of airport planning but could only recommend airport relocation or other options. Small wonder that nothing was ever accomplished. My solution was to form a new government entity, the San Diego County Regional Airport Authority, which would assume the Port's airport operational duties and SANDAG's airport planning responsibility.

I made forming a San Diego County Regional Airport Authority my fifth goal. I asked District 2 council member Byron Wear, in whose council district the airport is located, to be my partner in this effort. In the spring of 2001, I presented my proposal for a San Diego County Regional Airport Authority to the Regional Government Efficiency Commission (RGEC). By summer, RGEC, chaired by Councilmember

Wear, recommended to state legislators the formation of a separate airport authority.

In the fall of 2001, State Senator Steve Peace and Assemblyman Howard Wayne led the effort to pass legislation forming the San Diego County Regional Airport Authority. The new government entity officially took over responsibility for operating the existing airport and building a new airport on December 31, 2002. I appointed retired Air Force Colonel Joe Craver, prominent land use attorney Paul Peterson, and San Diego City Councilmember Ralph Inzunza as the City of San Diego's first representatives on the airport authority. While the difficult process of selecting a new airport site still lay ahead, our establishing the Airport Authority created the mechanism to solve the airport problem and essentially complete my fifth goal.

By the end of my first two years as mayor, we had made great strides in achieving my first five goals:

Goal #1: The Ethics Commission was established and operating.

Goal #2: State Route 56 was on its way to completion in 2004.

Goal #3: The California Public Utility Commission had approved our expanded utility undergrounding program.

Goal #4: Sewer spills and beach closures had been dramatically reduced.

Goal #5: The San Diego County Regional Airport Authority had been created.

In my opinion, the key to our success was setting clear goals, asking others to help achieve those goals, and then sharing credit with them for successes. Most people prefer a leader who will work with them on deciding what to do and then empowering them to do it. I viewed my city council colleagues and City staff as partners, and that made all the difference.

Throwing out one of the first pitches at Petco Park on opening night (2004)

10

THE MAYORAL FIRST TERM:
Leadership With 2020 Vision

> "Leadership is the art of getting someone else to do
> something you want done because he wants to do it."
> —*Dwight D. Eisenhower*

DURING MY CAMPAIGN FOR MAYOR in 2000, I promised to provide "leadership with 2020 vision." And although this was a campaign slogan, I sincerely hoped to deliver on that promise. I intended to articulate and pursue a clear vision of how to improve San Diego's quality of life by the year 2020. The 10 goals were the vehicle to implement that vision.

The first five goals were enough to keep the mayor's office busy. And some people thought it would be counterproductive to attempt too much. Former San Diego Mayor Roger Hedgecock recommended selecting no more than three major goals. But I believed we could achieve more, and my partnership strategy hinged on having at least one shared goal with each of the eight city councilmembers and the city attorney. If I had guessed right, that teamwork could leverage our efforts on other issues. Why set limits on what we might achieve?

After meeting with city staff, councilmembers, and campaign supporters in December 2000, I eventually settled on five additional goals.

They were definitely not simple projects added to round out a wish list. In fact, some were among the toughest challenges the City faced at the time—challenges requiring extraordinary teamwork and financing. But as the new mayor, I felt I had to try.

GOAL #6:
Complete the Ballpark

In April 2004 the Padres opened their season for the first time in brand new Petco Park in downtown San Diego. The ballpark was packed with cheering fans, and dazzling floodlights illuminated a magnificent state-of-the-art facility. After the big reveal, Ann Jarmusch, the *San Diego Union-Tribune*'s architecture critic, wrote that the quality of its design "reflects San Diego in timeless and profound ways. We need more architecture of this caliber to knit this city together in body, mind and spirit."

Ironically, the much-praised ballpark had been very divisive and almost didn't get built at all. Even though San Diego voters had approved its construction in November 1998, the project lurched from one obstacle to another, from funding and historic site issues to stubborn opponents determined to stop it.

By the time I took office in December 2000, the ballpark project was a train wreck. The City and the Padres had started construction in 2000, but suspended all work in the early fall of 2000 when the City ran out of money because it had been unable to issue bonds to pay for its share. The ballpark site consisted of numerous concrete pilings and rusting rebar jutting from a huge hole in the ground—sort of a 21st century Stonehenge. So I made completion of the ballpark my sixth goal.

The City's effort to issue bonds to pay its share of the ballpark costs had derailed for three reasons. First, the FBI was investigating whether San Diego City Councilmember Valerie Stallings had a conflict of interest when she voted for the ballpark project. Second, ballpark financing was dependent on hotel transient occupancy taxes from the construction of a major waterfront hotel that had been delayed by environmental issues. Third, multiple anti-ballpark lawsuits had created uncertainties that made Wall Street skittish about selling the bonds.

The first problem was that all the ballpark agreements between the City and the Padres might be invalid if Councilmember Stallings had a conflict of interest when she voted to approve them. Finally, after months of investigation, the U.S. Attorney exonerated San Diego Padres owner John Moores of any wrongdoing, but found that Councilmember Stallings had received gifts from the Padres owner, neglected to disclose the gifts as legally required, and failed to disqualify herself from voting on matters relating to the Padres. Stallings pled guilty to two misdemeanors and resigned from the San Diego City Council.

After Stallings's resignation, the new city council voted to approve all the prior agreements between the City and the Padres, thereby removing any taint from the involvement of Stallings in previous city council ballpark votes. The City then filed a validation action—a lawsuit aimed at getting the courts to validate the council action. In June 2001 Judge Judith McConnell ruled that the City had acted lawfully when it readopted the ballpark agreements, which precluded future lawsuits contesting the validity of the ballpark contracts.

The second problem was that the financing plan for the City's contribution to the ballpark project was no longer workable. The new ballpark was expected to cost $450 million. The City's contribution was to be $225 million, paid for with bonds the City would issue. The City bonds were to be repaid annually from hotel transient occupancy taxes, but one-third of the projected hotel tax revenues was to come from the construction of a major waterfront hotel that had been delayed indefinitely by environmental problems.

Thanks to some innovative thinking by the San Diego City Attorney's Office, the San Diego City Manager's staff, and the Centre City Development Corporation (CCDC), we developed a restructured financing plan for the ballpark. We were able to significantly reduce the City contribution to the project from its hotel transient occupancy taxes by dramatically increasing the City's downtown redevelopment agency's (CCDC's) contribution from downtown property tax revenues. Not only did the revised plan please the bond underwriters, it also reduced the impact of the ballpark project on the City's general fund used to pay for police, fire, parks, libraries, and other municipal services.

The final and most frustrating problem that the City faced was the multitude of anti-ballpark lawsuits, many filed by former San Diego City Councilmember Bruce Henderson. Since Henderson had asked me to preside over his marriage when I was a judge, and I had obliged, I assumed his opposition to the ballpark wasn't personal. Nevertheless, his anti-ballpark crusade gave me a huge headache. The bond underwriters and bond insurers were unwilling to proceed with the bond sale while any of the lawsuits were pending. Eventually the City Attorney's Office, with help from outside counsel, prevailed in every pending case. The city council approved the ballpark bond sale, which finally occurred in February 2002. Construction resumed within days.

The completion of the long-delayed ballpark was cause for great celebration, and if there was any apprehension remaining, it was only because I had been invited to throw out a pitch on opening night. My anxiety increased when I learned that former President Jimmy Carter and Commissioner of Major League Baseball Bud Selig would also be throwing out ceremonial pitches. The moment of truth arrived April 8, 2004, at the opening night ceremonies. Jimmy Carter set the standard. The 79-year-old former president stepped to the mound and fired a fastball. It was a strike. Bud Selig and I exchanged looks of amazement. When it was my turn, I threw a lob that sailed across the plate without a bounce. That was good enough for me. The moment had come and gone and to my relief, I had not humiliated myself. The Padres went on to beat the San Francisco Giants, sealing a perfect evening.

Looking back I would like to think that completion of the downtown ballpark was one of my major accomplishments as mayor. It saved Major League Baseball for San Diego. And it did far more. The ballpark project had always been intended to jump-start redevelopment of the neglected east side of downtown, just as Horton Plaza had done earlier for the center city area, but few anticipated how quickly it happened. No sooner had the ballpark opened than development took off. Some projects—the hotels, condos, and offices immediately around the ballpark—were part of the overall plan for the project. But soon new construction was rising all around the East Village, the ballpark's immediate neighborhood.

A study commissioned by the San Diego Regional Economic Development Corporation found that by the end of 2009, Petco Park had spurred development of more than 3,500 residential units, almost 1,000 hotel rooms, and about 600,000 square feet of commercial space. The estimated market value was $1.79 billion.

Petco Park Opening Night, April 8, 2004—(left to right) Former Padre Dave Winfield, Mayor Murphy, President Jimmy Carter, Baseball Commissioner Bud Selig, San Diego Padres owner John Moores

I was flattered that Padres owner John Moores gave me a share of credit for this phase of downtown redevelopment. In the May 2005 issue of San Diego magazine, he was quoted as saying, "Without Dick Murphy's leadership in putting the financing in place for the city's portion of the new ballpark, there would be no Petco Park, the continuing downtown renaissance would not have happened." But in reality, he should have patted himself on the back, too. Completion of the ballpark demanded a monumental commitment and tremendous patience from the team owner. The project succeeded because of Moores and a team effort from many others, including a creative CCDC staff and board; dedicated San Diego City attorneys, particularly Les Girard; a talented City Manager's staff; a visionary city council; and vocal support from the media and public. A lot of people "played ball" to transform and revitalize East Village—and, because of that, we all came out winners.

Goal #7:
Build a Library System

As mayor, I believed that building a new central library was important to creating a city worthy of our affection. I was hardly the first mayor to promote that idea. The old main library at Eighth and E downtown, which opened in 1954, had been an object of scorn for years. It was small and unattractive—even by the standards of the 1950s. It had aged poorly. The roof leaked, and water pipes burst, damaging books. Rooms intended for public use had to be converted to storage. Simply put, the main library had become a civic embarrassment. Meanwhile, major cities across America, among them Seattle, Chicago, and Salt Lake City, built main libraries that became architectural icons and cultural centers for their citizens.

Over the years, a whole series of central library proposals raised hopes, only to fall apart. A plan for a grand library on the bay collapsed because of resistance from the San Diego Unified Port District. The city council actually bought the old Sears site in Hillcrest for a central library but quickly—and mercifully, in my opinion—resold the land to developers for housing and commercial businesses. The Hillcrest location would have presented parking issues, as it does for its present users and, besides, a main library really belongs downtown. The City's redevelopment agency invested in another downtown library site, this time on a block on Kettner Boulevard, but eventually this location also was rejected. The City finally settled on a site in the less developed east side of downtown San Diego.

When I became mayor, I wanted to figure out a strategy to put the main library on the road to development once and for all. It was not going to be easy. The fact that so many plans for this project wound up in a trash heap indicated that the city council paid lip service to the idea but felt no deep commitment to actually getting the job done.

I blamed the failure mostly on the district-only elections, which caused many councilmembers to believe that neighborhood libraries in their districts were more important than a new central library. Somehow, they were convinced that the library system could prosper if it consisted of all branches and not much of a trunk. The City's librarians did not agree, nor did I. So I joined forces with newly elected District 7 Councilmember Jim Madaffer, who had a long history as a library supporter. I asked for his help in building a comprehensive library system as Goal #7.

I knew I could count on Councilmember Byron Wear, whose council district included downtown, to support a new main library. But to assure approval, we needed an approach that would appeal to all councilmembers.

Working with then Library Director Anna Tatár and her staff, we proposed and the city council approved a $300 million plan for a library

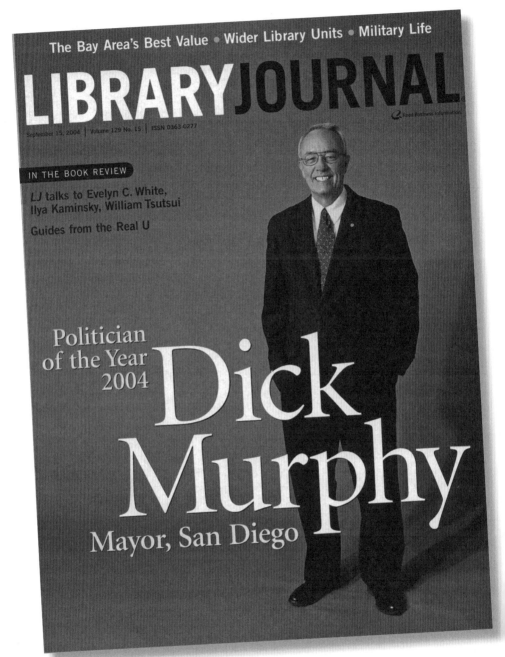

Library Journal *Politician of the Year (2004)*
(© 2004 Library Journal)

system for the 21st century. It included both $150 million for a new central library and $150 million for branch libraries in each council district. Under the proposal, every councilmember's district would get a new branch library or upgrade. The plan was therefore approved easily. As a result of the 21st Century Library Plan, I was selected Politician of the Year in 2004 by *Library Journal* magazine—and even made the front cover.

The plan quickly spurred development of several branches. Using a combination of developer fees, redevelopment funds, state grants, and charitable donations, we expanded or built new libraries in Mission Valley, Point Loma, Barrio Logan, Serra Mesa, La Jolla, Otay Mesa, College/Rolando, and North University City.

I had hoped at least to start construction of the new central library during my time as mayor. The City owned the building site at Park Boulevard and J Street downtown. The architectural designs by Rob Wellington Quigley and Tucker Sadler & Associates were complete. State Senator Dede Alpert had obtained a state grant of $20 million for the library. I had twisted arms at the Centre City Development Corporation to get a commitment for $80 million in funding for the project. The Library Foundation had pledged to raise the remaining $50 million. Unfortunately, the City's financial uncertainties arising from the pension fund debacle delayed the start of construction.

The long-awaited groundbreaking for the new central library finally took place in June 2010. I attended, witnessing the fruition of my efforts. Nevertheless, there were still questions about finding enough funding to complete construction, now estimated to cost $185 million by the time the library is completed in 2013.

Had I still been mayor, I would have turned immediately to the Centre City Development Corporation for additional financial help. The ballpark and surrounding East Village developments are generating millions in new property tax revenues. I can't think of a better way to use that money than to help finish the main library in a once – blighted section of East Village and make it the jewel that all San Diegans deserve.

GOAL #8:
Make San Diego America's Safest City

Because the most important service that local government provides is public safety, I included making San Diego America's safest city as my eighth goal. Initially I partnered with District 4 Councilmember George Stevens and later Councilmember Charles Lewis, who represented the city's southeastern communities, to focus on fighting crime. Thanks to the leadership of police chiefs David Bejarano and Bill Lansdowne, San Diego had the lowest violent crime rate among the 10 largest U.S. cities during 2002 and 2003. Goal #8 had essentially been achieved.

An unexpected disaster, however, the devastating Cedar Fire, persuaded me to expand this goal to include fire protection. As it turned out, there were many lessons to be learned from the worst wildfire in San Diego history.

A lost hunter had lit a signal fire that started the conflagration south of Ramona in the late afternoon of Oct. 23, 2003. The next morning, I awoke to a call from San Diego Assistant Fire Chief Augie Ghio, alerting me that the fire was raging out of control. It was moving from the eastern portion of San Diego County and heading toward the City of San Diego. San Diego Fire Chief Jeff Bowman, City Manager Mike Uberuaga, and I went up in a helicopter that morning to survey the disaster scene. Below, the skies were filled with smoke as towering flames raced across the landscape. Whipped by fierce Santa Ana winds, the advancing line of fire sped forward, charring everything in its path.

The flames soon reached the City of San Diego communities of Scripps Ranch and Tierrasanta, and as embers showered on homes, many exploded into flames. The San Diego Fire Department struggled valiantly against overwhelming odds. Finally, the crews got a break when the winds shifted, improving firefighting conditions and enabling them to gain control.

The disaster was so widespread and severe that San Diego County received a federal disaster declaration, enabling federal assistance for its local governments, agencies, and tribes as well as individuals who suffered wildfire losses. Michael Brown—yes, the same FEMA director who would be criticized and sent packing two years later for the slow response to Hurricane Katrina—was quick to provide the help we requested for the City of San Diego. I asked him to establish a disaster assistance center in Scripps Ranch, the most fire-damaged area of the city. The request was fulfilled promptly, which was a boon to San Diego citizens who had lost their homes and needed aid and information.

The Cedar Fire destroyed a total of 2,820 homes countywide, but according to the City's after-action report, about 320 of those homes were within City of San Diego boundaries. It could have been worse, especially considering the San Diego Fire Department's limited personnel and resources. When the big fire struck, the department did not even have its full complement of firefighters available in its own jurisdiction. Some had been deployed to fight wildfires outside San Diego County that had broken out shortly before the Cedar Fire erupted.

Once the hellish Santa Ana winds died down and shifted in favor of the firefighters, there was no mistaking the message. Nature had given a frightening demonstration of its power. We needed to ensure that we were better prepared for the next big wildfire.

Working with Fire Chief Jeff Bowman and newly elected District 2 Councilmember Michael Zucchet, the former firefighters union political director, we adopted a Five Point Plan to improve fire preparedness:

- Toughening building codes to make houses more fire-resistant, including banning new wood shake roofs

- Strengthening brush management by providing and encouraging defensible space around structures
- Upgrading firefighting equipment by purchasing 15 new firefighting vehicles
- Increasing firefighting personnel, a goal that fiscal constraints prevented
- Implementing year-round aerial firefighting by purchasing San Diego's first fire-rescue helicopter

Our biggest success was the purchase of San Diego's first fire-rescue helicopter—Copter One. Given the City's fiscal problems in 2004, it was a challenge to find the $3 million needed to purchase a helicopter. Eventually I managed to convince the Center City Development Corporation to repay a $3 million loan from the City, and that secured the funding. The fire-rescue helicopter is a valuable asset, facilitating rescues and snuffing out many fires before they spread. But no matter how much the City prepares, it will always be vulnerable to a major wildfire.

GOAL #9:
Pursue Energy Independence

At the time of my inauguration, the State of California's energy deregulation policies had created an energy crisis. Energy shortages were causing skyrocketing energy bills and rolling blackouts that were threatening the economy and individual financial security. The crisis provided an opportunity to purse energy independence as my ninth goal. We first created the position of "city energy czar" to seek ways for the City to conserve energy and utilize renewable resources such as solar energy.

Working with the City's Environmental Services Department, led by Rich Hayes, we launched a series of actions to make San Diego a model city in energy conservation and utilization of renewable resources:

- The City constructed its first energy-independent building, using solar panels to generate all of the building's electrical needs.
- The City converted its traffic lights to light-emitting diodes, saving millions of kilowatts of electricity annually.
- The City brought online the world's first wastewater hydro-electric power plant, generating electricity by running treated sewage effluent through a turbine (so-called "poop to power").
- The city council adopted the U.S. Green Building Council's Leadership in Energy and Environmental Design (LEED) standard for all new and renovated City facilities.
- Working with District 6 Councilmember Donna Frye, we established a Sustainable Energy Advisory Board to promote the use of solar power and other renewable energy resources in both the public and private sectors of the San Diego.

This goal was ambitious. The plan's objective was to free San Diego from the whims of the power market, fight global warming by reducing carbon dioxide emissions, and enhance national security by lessening our dependence on imported fossil fuels. I was honored by America's Republicans for Environmental Protection with its 2003 Theodore Roosevelt Award for this effort.

GOAL #10:
Develop a San Diego River Park

Having formerly been chair of the city Park and Recreation Board, I wanted to include expanding park opportunities as my tenth goal. Initially we called for completing San Diego's Multiple Species Conservation Plan (MSCP), the city's 50,000-acre open space and habitat conservation system. And during my first term as mayor, working with Park and Recreation Director Ellie Oppenheim and her staff, we added some 3,000 acres to the MSCP.

However, we soon focused on a new project: developing a San Diego River Park along the San Diego River from the Pacific Ocean to the river's headwaters in the mountains of the Cleveland National Forest. Although the river runs through the middle of the city and is of particular ecological and historic significance, it had been ignored for decades. In 2002, to pursue that vision, I convened the San Diego River Alliance, a multijurisdictional coalition of elected officials from the City of San Diego, the City of Santee, San Diego County, the California State Legislature, and the U.S. Congress. As a start, in 2002 we convinced the San Diego City Council to fund the preparation of a San Diego River Park Master Plan in the city.

Seeking a reliable source of funding for the San Diego River Park, I worked with Assemblymember Christine Kehoe in 2002 to create the San Diego River Conservancy, a state agency to fund preservation and restoration of the river. On the day Governor Gray Davis signed the bill creating the conservancy, he gave us a check for $12 million. As the first chair of the San Diego River Conservancy during 2003 and 2004, my vision was to develop a master plan for the park and acquire key parcels in the riparian corridor so that one day San Diegans would be able to hike or paddle the entire 52-mile length of the San Diego River.

When I unveiled my 10 goals, I was pleased with the immediate positive reception. The media praised the goals, and the city manager and his staff pledged to help make them a reality. By the end of two years, we had made significant progress in achieving my second five goals:

Goal #6: The downtown ballpark was back on track and expected to be completed in 2004.

Goal #7: A $300 million plan to build a new main library and branch libraries had been adopted.

Goal #8: San Diego had the lowest violent crime rate among the 10 largest cities in America.

Goal #9: The City's effort to promote solar power and other renewable energy sources had been launched.

Goal #10: The City was developing a draft master plan for a San Diego RiverPark, and the San Diego River Conservancy had been created to fund it.

However, dark clouds were gathering on the horizon. The dot.com bubble collapse, as well as the post-9/11 recession, reduced City tax revenues and put a strain on City finances. Funding problems with the City's pension system were beginning to surface. Unfortunately, we did not foresee the scope and fury of the approaching storm.

11

THE PENSION FUND DEFICIT:
First Wave of
a National Tsunami

*"San Diego's pension problems have given the city a bad name nationally,
but it's becoming more apparent every week that similar
benefit levels and funding shortfalls are plaguing governments
small and large across the nation."*
—*San Diego Union-Tribune*, December 27, 2010

GIVEN THE POLITICAL CLIMATE IN 2011, it is hard to believe there was a time when pension plans for public employees were thought to be good, even noble. A few decades ago, it was accepted that people who devoted their careers to public service deserved a pension—maybe not a fortune, but enough to let them live out their last years with dignity. For government managers, a solid pension plan also helped recruit and keep skilled, competent workers. At least, that was how it seemed when the economy was booming and the stock market was bullish.

During recent recessions, when millions of Americans lost their jobs and governments at all levels wrestled with huge budget deficits, serious pension fund troubles emerged in cities, counties, and states around the country, and public perception of this benefit soured. The plummeting stock market dragged down government pension fund portfolios, creating pension fund shortfalls and exposing the mistakes and vulnerabilities that had previously been submerged beneath public consciousness and out of the media spotlight.

That was what happened in San Diego, where the extent of the City's pension fund deficits began surfacing during the economic downturn of 2001 and 2002. San Diego was among the first cities in the 21st century to detect endemic problems and try to deal with them, and for our troubles, we were relentlessly vilified. As mayor, I found myself trying to fix our listing ship of state while fending off a steady stream of media attacks and trumped-up investigations. As far as I was concerned, these attacks were undeserved. San Diego wasn't "Enron by the Sea," a moniker still occasionally dredged up to smear the City. There never was any corruption—just mismanagement of the City's pension system for many years. The city managers and their staff members were honest and competent, and trying to do what they thought was best for the City. But they were not infallible.

It must be acknowledged that serious mistakes were made in San Diego over the course of the two decades before the problem surfaced. For instance, some benefits were enhanced and then applied retroactively, which added significantly to the pension fund's financial burden. Much of the problematic decision-making happened before I came into office as mayor. However, I voted for the city manager's pension fund proposal in 2002. I wish I could take back that vote. It only worsened San Diego's growing pension fund deficit, although I didn't realize it at the time.

Those of us on the council had relied on City staff members to guide us through the arcane actuarial tables, pension formulas, and projections. Later, it became clear that the mayor and council did not fully understand the complexities of the City's pension system or the pitfalls inherent in the city manager's recommendations, which we could have—and should have—challenged.

The *San Diego Union-Tribune* harshly blamed the City staff, stating in a July 2004 editorial that "successive city managers were the architects of this fiscal calamity, although it also was approved by an unwitting City Council."

The editorial made a valid point, but as elected officials of the City of San Diego, we were still accountable to the public and to our City employees. We learned a lesson the hard way: You can delegate authority, but you cannot completely delegate responsibility.

Ultimately, councilmembers studied and grasped the nature of the problem and began the difficult process of remedying the pension fund deficits. Understanding what had happened helped us move ahead with several reforms.

MP1 and the Corbett Settlement

One can trace the beginning of San Diego City's pension funding short-fall to the late 1970s when the City started making supplemental pension payments from "surplus" pension fund earnings to City retirees called the "13th check." At first, the 13th check was intended as a humane measure limited to City retirees who had very meager benefits. Eventually, it was made available to most retirees. This was not a wise practice, since the extra cash generated by pension fund investments in good times was supposed to make up for lower revenues during economic downturns.

And in the 1980s, the City started paying retirees' health care benefits from pension fund assets. The change occurred after the City withdrew from the Medicare and Social Security systems, a popular move that in the short term saved money for both the City and its employees. But that shifted to the City the burden of retiree health care, which turned out to be a big-ticket item. Together, the 13th check program and retiree health care benefits depleted pension fund assets by more than $100 million over the past three decades.

While these early steps adversely impacted funding of the City pension system, it was Manager's Proposal #1 ("MP1") in 1996 that brought about the first substantial erosion in the pension system's funding status.

In the spring of 1996, while Susan Golding was mayor and Jack McGrory was city manager, the City significantly increased retirement benefits for its employees.

First, the multiplier for most non-public safety employees was increased from 1.45 percent to 2.00 percent. Annual pension payments are calculated by multiplying the multiplier times employee annual salary times years of service. For example, prior to 1996, an employee who earned $40,000 after working for the City for 20 years would receive a pension of $11,600 annually. After the higher multiplier went into effect in 1996, that same employee's pension would increase to $16,000.

In addition to the increase in the formula for calculating basic pension benefits, the City in 1996 expanded the Purchase Service Credit benefit and added a Deferred Retirement Option Plan ("DROP"). The Purchase Service Credit permits City employees to purchase up to five years of service toward retirement benefits. The DROP program allows City employees to retire and receive retirement benefits while continuing to work for the City while earning a full salary. Initially, these benefits were designed to retain valuable, highly experienced employees but were extended to other City employees as well.

As a condition for providing the enhanced retirement benefits, the city manager required that the pension board of directors permit the City to contribute less than the actuarially required contribution to the pension system for 10 years. This was later referred to as Manager's Proposal #1 or MP1. MP1 included a "trigger" provision that required the City to pay the pension system whatever was necessary to prevent the system's funding ratio (pension assets divided by pension liabilities) from falling below 82.3 percent. The city council and the pension board approved MP1 in 1996.

There were three major flaws in Manager's Proposal #1. First, the most obvious defect was that the City's contribution shortfall to the pension system between fiscal year 1997 and fiscal year 2006 was projected to exceed $100 million. Second, the increase in the formula for calculating pension benefits was retroactive for an employee's prior years of service, resulting in an immediate $77 million increase in the City's pension obligations. Third, the "trigger" mechanism created a risk that the City would face a substantial balloon payment should the system experience significant investment losses (which it did in 2001 and 2002).

The second substantial erosion in the pension system's funding status was the Corbett Settlement in the spring of 2000. At this time, Susan Golding was still mayor, but Mike Uberuaga had replaced Jack McGrory as city manager. In a 1997 lawsuit involving Ventura County, the California Supreme Court had ruled that public employee compensation for the purpose of determining pension benefits should include not only base salary but also overtime pay and accrued leave.

In 1998 a class action lawsuit, *Corbett v. City Employee Retirement System*, was filed against the San Diego pension system, alleging that the pension system had miscalculated retirement benefits for City retirees by omitting overtime pay and accrued leave. Facing a potential liability to the pension system of hundreds of millions of dollars, a settlement was reached that gave:

- Retired employees a 7 percent one time benefit increase
- Active police and fire employees an enhanced multiplier of 3 percent (multiplied by salary times service years)
- Active other employees an enhanced multiplier from 2 percent to 2.25 percent (multiplied by salary times service years)

While the financial impact on the City of the settlement was less than the potential exposure from an adverse judgment, the settlement created significant fiscal risks for the future. Like MP1, the increase in the formula for calculating pension benefits was retroactive for an employee's prior years of service, resulting in another huge increase in the City's pension obligations. The Towers-Perrin Report, prepared by the city manager in 2003, concluded that the Corbett Settlement had increased unfunded liabilities of the pension system by 18 percent.

Manager's Proposal 2

When I took office as mayor in December 2000, neither I nor any of the newcity councilmembers had any idea that we had inherited a ticking time bomb. In fact, it is doubtful that the prior mayor and council fully understood that, either. The stock market boom of the late 1990s had generated enormous pension system investment gains that had masked the effect of increased pension benefits along with reduced pension contributions to the system by the city.

The first inkling that the mayor and council had of any problem with the pension system was a recommendation in late February 2002 from my Blue Ribbon Committee. The previous April I had appointed a nine-member citizens' committee to examine the City's fiscal health. The Blue Ribbon Committee made ten recommendations, one of which was that the City should fully fund the actuarially determined cost of the retirement system. The city council asked pension system staff to evaluate the recommendation.

It was not until spring 2002 that the city manager's office advised the mayor and council that the dot.com stock market crash was having a detrimental effect on the pension system's funding status. The city manager's office told us that the City could face a major financial crisis if the pension system-funding ratio fell below 82.3 percent. We were warned that MP1 might require the City to make a lump-sum payment to the pension system in the hundreds of millions of dollars.

At the same time, the post-911 recession was substantially reducing San Diego's tax revenues. In order to avoid employee layoffs, the non-public safety labor unions proposed to forego a pay raise in fiscal year 2002–2003 if the City would increase their members' pension multiplier from 2.25 percent to 2.5 percent. Other government jurisdictions in California had been granting similar increases (e.g., San Diego County grew to 3 percent). The city manager's office recommended the union's proposal as a way to help balance the City budget and stay competitive with other government employers.

The city manager's labor proposal was initially contingent on the pension board agreeing to:

- lower the trigger from 82.3 to 75 percent, and
- allow the City five years to ramp-up pension payments to the full actuarial rate if the new floor was breached (called "Manager's Proposal #2" or "MP2").

However, on advice of its actuary and fiduciary counsel, the 13-member pension board rejected the city manager's proposal. With time running out to complete labor negotiations before the City budget had to be adopted on June 30, 2002, the city council approved the increased pension multiplier in lieu of a pay raise.

After labor negotiations had concluded and the new fiscal year had begun on July 1, 2002, the city manager's office and the city attorney's office jointly recommended a revised proposal. The revised MP2 proposed to keep the trigger at 82.3 percent, but double the City's annual increase in contributions to the pension system in exchange for the pension board agreeing to the five-year ramp-up to full actuarial funding if the trigger was activated. With approval this time from the pension system's fiduciary counsel, the pension board approved the revised MP2.

While Manager's Proposal #2 averted the fiscal crisis of the City having to make a lump-sum payment of hundreds of millions of dollars to the pension system, it was still a mistake in retrospect. At the time, we thought doubling the City's annual increase in its pension contributions was very positive. We later realized that although it helped improve the state of the pension fund, it was still less than the actuarially required contribution and continued to underfund the system. While several reports prepared by the city estimated that the underfunding attributed to MP1 and MP2 only caused 10 percent of the pension funding shortfall, the City should have begun paying the actuarially required contribution in July 2002.

The more serious mistake in Manager's Proposal #2 was increasing the pension multiplier from 2.25 percent to 2.5 percent. While the prior pension benefit increases in MP1 in 1996 and the Corbett Settlement in 2000 were the primary causes of the pension deficit, our increase of the multiplier in 2002 added to the pension funding shortfall. The error would not have been so serious if the increase in the multiplier had been

At a San Diego City Council meeting with City Manager Mike Uberuaga (2003)
(Credit: The San Diego Union-Tribune/ZUMAPRESS.com)

prospective from the date it took effect. The fatal mistake was making the increase retroactive for an employee's prior years of service.

Addressing the Pension Fund Deficit

In January 2003 a class action lawsuit was filed against the City. *Gleason vs. City of San Diego* alleged that the City's failure to pay the full actuarially required contribution to the pension system violated both the city charter and municipal code. Initially the city attorney's office advised the mayor and council that the lawsuit had no merit. We were further advised not to take any action to address the pension under-funding for fear of compromising the litigation.

In February 2003 the pension system staff finally responded to the city council's request to evaluate the Blue Ribbon Committee's recommendation regarding funding of the pension system. Pension staff attributed the delay in providing the report to the need to have the fiscal year 2002 actuarial evaluation prior to responding. Staff reported that the June 30, 2002, actuarial evaluation showed that pension fund assets had declined to $2.5 billion, while pension fund liabilities had increased to $3.2 billion. That resulted in an unfunded liability of more than $700 million and a funding ratio of 77 percent.

The mayor and council were initially told that the primary cause of the funding shortfall was the dramatic decline in the securities markets in which the pension fund had invested most of its assets. It was also pointed out that most public and private pension systems nationwide were experiencing the same funding declines. While it was true that investment losses were a significant contributor to the unfunded pension liability, we subsequently learned there were other major causes:

- Benefit increases from 1996, 2002, and Corbett
- Underfunding from MP1 and MP2
- Fund diversions to pay retirees' health care and the 13th check

In light of the unsettling report made by pension system staff in February 2003, the City Council Rules Committee that I chaired asked the city manager to provide a report on measures to take before the situation further deteriorated. However, the city attorney's office convinced the city manager not to make a report for fear it would compromise the Gleason litigation. Furthermore, it was pointed out to the mayor and council that the City could not legally modify any pension benefits until the current labor agreement expired in June 2005.

Frustrated by the City's seeming inability to meaningfully address the pension funding problem, I created a citizen's Pension Reform Commission in September 2003 to analyze the pension funding problem and recommend solutions. It was a good government move because the nine-member commission drawn from accounting, law, and other fields ferreted out the causes of the pension deficit and made a number of helpful suggestions. But it was a political disaster because the commission's report was released shortly before the November 2004 mayoral election. The report was intended to be a plan to resolve the pension-funding problem, but most of the media treated it as an indictment of the City's handling of the situation.

By 2004 we had begun to make some progress in bolstering the financial stability of the pension system. In finally settling the Gleason litigation in August 2004, the City agreed to stop underfunding the pension fund and start paying the actuarially required contribution at the start of the next fiscal year, July 1, 2005. This ended a decade of underfunding which was one of the four main causes of the pension shortfall.

In response to the Pension Reform Commission recommendations, the City stopped using pension funds to pay retiree health benefits in late 2004. This ended another of the four main causes of the pension fund deficit. Also in response to the Pension Reform Commission recommendation, we restructured the Pension Board in 2004 so that a majority of its members would not be City employees or retirees.

During labor union negotiations in the spring of 2005, we began to address the third main cause of the pension funding shortfall—benefit increases. We eliminated the Deferred Retirement Option Program (DROP), the Purchase of Service Credits, and the 13th check for new employees hired after July 1, 2005. (We were advised that we could not legally eliminate those pension benefits for existing employees.) In addition, we froze salaries for two years and required increased employee contributions into the pension system. Unfortunately, the progress we were making was largely ignored by most of the media in favor of efforts to assign blame for the problem.

Pension Mania

The election of Michael Aguirre as city attorney in November 2004 exacerbated the situation. Immediately after he took office, he proceeded

At a news conference discussing pension issues (2004)
(Credit: The San Diego Union-Tribune/ZUMAPRESS.com)

to accuse City leaders of securities fraud and conflict of interest. Much of the media encouraged a lynch mob mentality.

As a Superior Court judge, I had very high regard for the San Diego County District Attorney's office. But the DA's office got caught up in the hysteria and accused six pension board members of a conflict of interest. After years of defamatory headlines and legal expenses, the California Supreme Court threw out the cases and exonerated the falsely accused pension board members.

The United States Attorney's office also joined the witch hunt and brought criminal charges against several pension system staff and board members. They were accused of violating the federal "Honest Services Law." The U.S. District Court in San Diego also eventually dismissed the case for lack of merit.

The United States Securities and Exchange Commission (SEC) filed a civil (not criminal) action against the former city manager, the former city auditor, and several members of their staffs. The lawsuit alleged failure of the City to adequately disclose pension funding issues in its bond offerings. (The SEC never accused the mayor or city council of securities law violations.) The U.S. District Court in San Diego threw out the securities fraud allegation. The defendants eventually admitted negligent misrepresentation and paid a fine. When you consider that all bond payments were paid and no investor lost any money, you have to wonder if SEC resources would have been better spent investigating Bernie Madoff.

Also ignored was the fact that San Diego was not the only municipality facing serious pension deficit problems. In the 2010 study, "The Crisis in Local Government Pensions," the authors point out that three dozen large cities in America, including New York, Chicago, Boston, and Philadelphia, have pension systems in worse shape than San Diego. But if you only listened to the local media, you would have thought that San Diego's pension problem was unique. More recently, reporters have finally focused on the obvious. The City of San Diego wasn't unique at all. As it turned out, the pension problems experienced in San Diego were happening elsewhere. They simply hadn't made headlines yet.

In an article published on December 27, 2010, the *San Diego Union-Tribune* finally acknowledged the obvious: "San Diego's pension problems have given the city a bad name nationally, but it's becoming more apparent every week that similar benefit levels and funding shortfalls are plaguing governments small and large across the nation."

The San Diego Union-Tribune • Sunday, February 29, 2004

Steve Breen THE SAN DIEGO UNION-TRIBUNE

(Credit: The San Diego Union-Tribune)

12

THE 2004 MAYORAL ELECTION:
Murphy's Law Prevails

"Anything that can go wrong, will go wrong."
—Murphy's Law

WHEN I RAN FOR MAYOR IN 2000, I expected to serve only one term. My intention was to set some goals for the City, achieve those goals during my first term as mayor, and not seek reelection. The plan was somewhat liberating. I felt free to vote my conscience on the city council without worrying about the political consequences.

My initial instincts were confirmed by personal events during 2002. My beloved mother passed away at age 90—reminding me that our time on earth is limited. My youngest daughter, Kelly, graduated from college. My son, Brian, and daughter, Shannon, both were married. And I turned 60. It seemed like a good time to move on and pursue other interests.

The Decision to Run for Reelection

After considerable ambivalence, I announced in March 2003 that I would not seek reelection. I was somewhat taken aback by an avalanche of requests for me to reconsider. Some said I owed it to San Diego to finish the projects that I had started. Others told me that my reelection would be easy, showing me a poll that indicated that I had a 70 percent approval rating.

At the time, the *San Diego Union-Tribune* newspaper editorialized:

> Mayor Dick Murphy's abrupt decision to abandon his bid for reelection comes as a stunning disappointment. San Diego needs his steady, no-nonsense leadership. The mayor is widely respected, often admired, a rare happenstance in politics today. Because of his popularity, he faced no significant opposition in his re-election campaign.

Against my better judgment, in April 2003 I relented and agreed to seek reelection.

The 2004 Mayoral Primary Election

Not long after that, events began taking a sudden, often unexpected, turn for the worse. Just one month after I had announced I would run again, the U.S. Attorney's office raided the city council offices of Councilmembers Ralph Inzunza, Charles Lewis, and Michael Zucchet. In August 2003 they were indicted for allegedly accepting campaign contributions in exchange for agreeing to try to repeal a City ordinance that prohibited touching between patrons and strippers at nude entertainment establishments.

Although neither the mayor nor any of the rest of the city councilmembers was implicated in any way, the indictments resulted in sensational headlines that tainted the entire city council. Reporters were all over allegations that evoked tabloid images of salacious activity and tawdry backroom deals. The truth apparently proved less interesting to them.

Later, the *Los Angeles Times* wrote that "when the case burst into public view, it hinted at a culture of corruption at the San Diego City Hall." The same article acknowledged that, as the case unwound, it appeared the furor had been vastly overblown. "The case proved to be built on weak evidence, a strained interpretation of the law, and questionable conduct by federal prosecutors. The contributions had been reported on the council members' financial disclosure forms. And no repeal of the law was ever introduced."

Zucchet was ultimately acquitted. Lewis died before trial. And Inzunza was convicted for violating a federal law that several federal courts subsequently found to be unconstitutional.

Nevertheless, first impressions of this case caused collateral damage for innocent City Hall bystanders, including me as mayor. In the eyes of my potential rivals, I had gone from invincible to vulnerable. Soon after Inzunza, Lewis, and Zucchet were indicted, one of my 2000 mayoral primary opponents, Peter Q. Davis, announced he was again running for mayor.

The Cedar Fire in October 2003 further undermined the public's confidence in City government. The biggest fire in San Diego County history burned some 250,000 acres, including parts of the communities of Scripps Ranch and Tierrasanta in the City of San Diego. While most of the fire burned outside city limits, and the City did a good job fighting an unforeseen cataclysmic firestorm, there is always plenty of second-guessing and finger-pointing after a natural disaster, and San Diego was no exception. Shortly after the Cedar Fire, my 2000 mayoral election runoff opponent, San Diego County Supervisor Ron Roberts, jumped into the race.

By early 2004, the City pension system (see Chapter 11) had become a big issue in the mayor's race. However, it was the City's supplemental disclosure to the Securities and Exchange Commission in late January

2004 that was particularly damaging. In mid-January 2004 the city manager and city controller advised the mayor and council that City financial statements contained accounting errors and that the City needed to file a supplemental disclosure with the SEC regarding the errors. The timing could not have been worse.

Although the voluntary disclosure demonstrated that the City was not trying to cover up anything, it still triggered downgrades of the City's credit rating and prompted an investigation by the U.S. Attorney's office and the Securities and Exchange Commission. The City Controller's office had prepared the faulty financial statements. The City Manager's office had prepared the questionable bond disclosures. Even though the mayor and council had not approved the financial statements or been involved in preparing the bond disclosures, we were still blamed.

However, there was no time for regret over events beyond our control. I had made a decision to run again, and I was going to give it my best effort. We put together a crackerjack 2004 election campaign team. Campaign consultant Jennifer Tierney deftly handled the television advertising and mass mailings. Kelli Medina ran a very successful fundraising effort. And with approval from the Fair Political Practices Commission, my youngest daughter, Kelly, became the campaign coordinator. She ran our campaign headquarters and organized a terrific grassroots campaign. But due to the constant flow of negative publicity, my campaign workers found themselves constantly swimming upstream.

A week before the March 2004 primary election, the polls showed me capturing 33 percent of the vote. Davis and Roberts were virtually tied for second with Davis at 15 percent, Roberts at 13 percent, and 36 percent undecided. As the incumbent front-runner in the primary, we made the tactical decision to run a positive campaign, pointing out what we had accomplished.

On the other hand, Davis and Roberts were challengers, and had to battle for a spot in the general election runoff race. If Davis had spent part of his large television budget to point out that Roberts' County government pension system also had a $1 billion deficit and that San Diego County government failed to provide any fire protection during the Cedar Fire, Davis would have beaten Roberts. But he did not.

I finished first in the primary with 40 percent of the vote, Roberts was second with 30 percent, and Davis came in third at 22 percent. Only the top two finishers would go on to the runoff. Davis was out.

The 2004 Mayoral General Election

In the months following the March 2004 primary, we accomplished a great deal. The City hired my choice for a new city manager, Lamont Ewell. We hired a new accounting firm, KPMG, to correct the City's financial statements. We agreed to stop underfunding the pension system, and we placed on the November 2004 ballot a measure to restructure the retirement board.

There were other important civic milestones as well. In April we dedicated the new downtown ballpark. In July we opened the long-

With mayoral Chief of Staff John Kern prior to announcing reelection bid (2003)
(Credit: The San Diego Union-Tribune/ZUMAPRESS)

delayed State Route 56 freeway. We ended the San Diego Chargers controversial ticket guarantee, in which the city had agreed in the late 1990s to buy unsold tickets to San Diego Charger's home football games. And we released a proposed master plan for the creation of the San Diego River Park.

Perhaps our biggest accomplishment in 2004 was placing on the November ballot my proposal for a "strong mayor" form of government. San Diego had a city manager form of government, under which the city manager was the Chief Executive Officer of the City and ran its daily operations. The mayor of San Diego was the chair of the city council, setting its agenda and presiding at council meetings, but had only one of nine council votes. While the city council could set City policy and hire and fire the city manager, the mayor and council were prohibited from interfering in the City manager's daily operations.

The shortcomings of a weak mayor system became painfully clear during the 2003 Cedar Fire, a fast-moving crisis that demanded strong leadership. I declared a state of emergency for the city, but understood that, strictly speaking, the mayor had no authority to declare one without approval from the entire city council. I held press conferences to provide information and reassure the public—but under what authority? I could not make decisions involving the fire department. Under the city charter, the city council had to make a request to the city manager, who, in turn, would contact the city's fire department. With events moving fast, the system was slow and unwieldy.

It seemed to me that if the public expected the mayor to be responsible for the state of the city, the public should give the mayor the authority to control its destiny. However, prior efforts by former San Diego mayors Pete Wilson, Maureen O'Connor, and Susan Golding to give the mayor more power had failed. But now the fiscal problems facing the city had put a spotlight on the fragmented authority at city hall. It seemed like the voters might be ready for change.

Using as a template a strong mayor proposal advocated by the Better Government Association chaired by George Mitrovich, I proposed a ballot initiative to switch from a city manager to a strong mayor form of government. It made the mayor rather than the city manager the City's CEO, with power to prepare the annual budget, hire and fire City department heads, and veto city council decisions. Because the mayor would no longer be on the city council, the council would choose a presiding officer and hire its own independent budget analyst.

Getting the city council to agree to a ballot measure to create a strong mayor form of government was no easy sell. While I wanted to add a ninth councilmember to take the mayor's place on the council, councilmembers balked because it would have required another round of city council district reapportionment. While I proposed needing six council votes to override a mayoral veto, councilmembers objected—especially with only eight members. After I reluctantly compromised by supporting an eight-member city council and a five-vote override, the council agreed to put my revised strong mayor proposal on the November 2004 ballot.

The *San Diego Union-Tribune* editorial in July 2004 summed up the situation when it stated:

> This week the City Council made one of the most important decisions in decades to put on the ballot a sweeping retooling of San Diego's timeworn municipal government . . . San Diego's current structure, known as a city manager form of government, is not up to the challenges confronting America's seventh largest city . . . [T]he city charter severely restricts the powers of the elected mayor and City Council.
>
> Under the plan put forth by Mayor Dick Murphy, city government would be divided into separate executive and legislative branches. At present, the mayor is a member of the City Council and largely a figurehead, with few executive powers. Murphy's

proposal would remove the mayor from the council and give him genuine executive authority.

With support from the press and a concerted effort by civic leaders, my strong mayor proposal was approved by the voters in the November 2004 election.

Unfortunately, our accomplishments of the summer were overshadowed by developments in the fall. The report of the Pension Reform Committee that *I had created* was released in September, and was highly critical of the City's handling of its pension fund. A report by the law firm that *the City had hired* to look into its bond disclosure practices chastised the City for accounting and disclosure errors, although it found no intentional wrongdoing. Credit reporting agencies responded by lowering the City's credit rating. It seemed like the City was being punished for its efforts to be transparent. By late September, our polls showed Murphy and Roberts in a dead heat, each favored by 40 percent of the voters.

In late September, San Diego City Councilmember Donna Frye surprised everyone by entering the mayoral campaign as a last-minute write-in candidate. At first, neither Roberts nor I took her candidacy very seriously. In fact, our campaign initially thought that her candidacy might help us by drawing more votes away from Roberts than me. But as Roberts' attacks on me became increasingly vitriolic, the better Frye seemed to do.

By the end of October, the polls showed a close race among all three candidates—each with approximately 30 percent of the vote. On election night, Frye confounded the pundits by running first with 35 percent of the vote. Murphy was a close second with 34 percent. Roberts trailed at 31 percent. However, there were thousands of absentee ballots that had not been counted on election night, so the election night results were far from conclusive.

Shortly after the election, Roberts' supporters filed lawsuits in state and federal courts alleging that Frye's write-in candidacy was illegal under the city charter and that the election results should be declared null and void. The legal imbroglio dragged on for weeks, leaving the election in doubt. The courts ultimately ruled against Roberts' supporters, holding that even if the city charter prohibited Frye's write-in candidacy, Roberts was barred from relief because he should have sued prior to the election.

Frye's legal victory was short-lived, however. When the absentee vote was finally tallied in late November, it turned out that I had actually beaten Frye by about 2,000 votes. Frye's supporters in turn requested a recount and sued the San Diego County Registrar of Voters and me, claiming that the registrar had improperly disallowed approximately 5,000 of Frye's write-in votes. The recount lasted for days, and the lawsuits continued for weeks, leaving the result of the election hanging in the balance.

Thanks to the good work of my attorney, Bob Ottilie, the trial courts ultimately rejected lawsuits by Frye's supporters to overturn my election victory. But it was a hollow victory. I had won with 34.5 percent of the vote—not exactly a mandate. Frye and her supporters were embittered. And I had spent thousands of dollars in legal fees and still faced mounting legal bills to oppose an appeal by Frye's supporters.

Resignation

In spite of all the controversy surrounding the 2004 mayoral election, I was determined to press forward in 2005 with an agenda to fix San Diego's financial problems. In my January 2005 State of the City address, I set forth a specific plan to reduce the City's pension deficit:

- Make the full actuarial payment to the pension system starting July 2005.
- Issue pension obligation bonds to repay previous underfunding.

- Impose a two-year salary freeze on City employees.
- Increase employees' annual contribution to the pension system.
- Eliminate the Deferred Retirement Option Plan (DROP) for new hires.

The pension deficit reduction plan required good faith negotiations with the City employees' labor unions in the spring of 2005 and incorporation into the San Diego's annual budget, which took effect on July 1, 2005. But before we could implement the plan, the situation rapidly deteriorated. The Securities and Exchange Commission stepped up its investigation into the pension system disclosures, issuing subpoenas for a sweeping array of documents. To be sure that no one accused us of covering up, my office devoted hundreds of hours in an effort to comply with the subpoenas.

The election of Mike Aguirre as San Diego city attorney in November 2004 made matters worse. Soon after his election, he accused the mayor and City Council of violating federal securities laws. While the U.S. Securities and Exchange Commission subsequently rejected Aguirre's accusations, Aguirre's unpredictable behavior caused constant turmoil inside City Hall that made it extremely difficult to solve the city's fiscal problems. Because it was impossible to work with an attorney we could not trust, the city was forced to hire an outside consultant to deal with the SEC investigation.

Most of the media had usually been fair and objective during my first term as mayor. But as my second term unfolded, some reporters abandoned any pretext of providing a balanced perspective on pension issues. The hostile press coverage eroded public confidence in City government, further inflaming an already-incendiary situation. Protesters camped out in my front yard, creating a security threat to my wife and family. I received death threats that at times required 24-hour police protection from my security detail, Jim Jarrett, Odie Gallop, and Tony Lessa.

By April of 2005, the post-election lawsuits, the SEC investigation, a recalcitrant city attorney, a hostile press, and security threats had all become a major distraction impeding my efforts to solve the City's financial problems. I finally concluded it would be best for San Diego if I resigned. I had reluctantly agreed to run for a second term because people convinced me that it would be in the city's best interest. But now it seemed that the city was no longer better served with me as mayor, that the honorable thing to do would be to step down and give the city a fresh start. God was pointing me toward the exit.

After I announced my resignation in April 2005, I stayed on as mayor for three months to approve the annual budget and participate in labor negotiations that would reduce the city's pension deficit. We succeeded in eliminating the DROP program, purchase of service credits, and payment of the 13th check for new employees hired after July 1, 2005. In addition, we implemented a wage freeze and increased pension

Announcing my resignation (2005) (Credit: The San Diego Union-Tribune/ZUMAPRESS.com)

fund contributions for existing employees. While our effort should have been applauded as a good start at reducing the pension deficit, the press dismissed it as too little, too late.

I have no regrets about running for mayor in 2000. It was a privilege and honor to be the 33rd mayor of America's seventh largest city at the start of the new millennium. God opened the door and I walked through it. Of course, I would have done a few things differently. If I had it to do over again, I certainly would not have run for reelection in 2004.

Could I have handled some matters more deftly? Possibly, but I wasn't sure how to do that without compromising my integrity. My temperament—probably better-suited to being a judge instead of a politician—would not allow me to throw people under the bus before they had their day in court. Politically speaking, it probably would have been more expedient to condemn the indicted city councilmembers or publicly criticize the members of the City's embattled pension board. But, in my mind, people are innocent until proven guilty, and I was not going to compromise that principle.

What I do regret is that the achievements during my tenure were drowned out by a cacophony of shrill outcries over the pension deficit. I tried to stay focused on my vision for San Diego—establishing an ethics commission, completing State Route 56, undergrounding overhead wires, reducing sewer spills, forming an airport authority, constructing the downtown ballpark, building a new main library, purchasing San Diego's first fire-rescue helicopter, promoting solar energy, and creating a San Diego River Park.

During my time as mayor, I strove to fulfill my 2000 election campaign promise to provide a clear vision of where San Diego should be in the year 2020. With the help of my fellow councilmembers, the city manager's staff, and my mayoral staff, we implemented much of that vision. But we did not foresee the pension deficit and its political fallout.

And along the way, my leadership with 2020 vision was blindsided by Murphy's Law: "Anything that can go wrong, will go wrong."

In the end, I would like to believe that I followed the advice of one of my heroes, Teddy Roosevelt, when he stated:

> It is not the critic who counts; not the man who points out how the strong man stumbles, or where the doer of deeds could have done them better. The credit belongs to the man who is actually in the arena, whose face is marred by dust and sweat and blood; who strives valiantly; who errs, and comes short again and again, because there is no effort without error or shortcoming; but who does actually strive to do the deeds; who knows the great enthusiasms, the great devotions; who spends himself in a worthy cause; who at the best knows in the end the triumph of high achievement, and who at the worst, if he fails, at least fails while daring greatly, so that his place shall never be with those cold and timid souls who know neither victory nor defeat.

The San Diego Union-Tribune • Sunday, November 24, 2002

Steve Breen THE SAN DIEGO UNION-TRIBUNE

Epilogue

Creating a City
Worthy of Our Affection

"San Diego has the location and the physical foundation
for an important, perhaps a great, city.
—John Nolen, 1908

IN THE EARLY 1900S, civic leader George Marston paid Massachusetts planner John Nolen to develop "a comprehensive plan" to guide the development of the City of San Diego. Nolen's plan inspired a succession of the city's leaders to continue shaping and building a grand West Coast city.

As San Diego's mayor in the first years of the 21st century, I also had a plan. During my tenure, I set 10 specific goals to create a city worthy of our affection. But as with all the mayors before me, I had only a limited number of years to move the city forward. And there is so much unfinished business, so many fresh ideas to explore. In this epilogue, I suggest 10 proposals to pursue during the next decade.

The City of San Diego faces another mayoral election in 2012 with no incumbent. The winner most likely will be mayor through the year 2020—during the 100th anniversary of the 1915 Exposition and the

250th birthday of the city and state. I would expect every serious mayoral candidate to spell out a specific vision for San Diego's future. My hope is that some of the following ideas might be included.

PROPOSAL #1:
Complete the San Diego River Park

The San Diego River should be an enormous historical and environmental resource. The river's headwaters flow some 52 miles from the pristine mountain wilderness of the Cleveland National Forest all the way to the Pacific Ocean. The river tumbles through Lakeside, Santee, and the City of San Diego. Along the way it provides a magnificent riparian habitat for numerous plant and animal species and scenic open space for public recreation.

The river is a key element in San Diego's history and culture. It was home to California's earliest inhabitants. For 10,000 years Native Americans lived along its banks. In 1769 the first Spanish settlement in California was built on a hill overlooking the river—today's Old Town San Diego. A few years later, California's first mission was located seven miles upstream adjacent to the river: the Mission San Diego de Alcala, still an active church. And farther upstream, California's first water project was constructed in the early 1800s—the Old Mission Dam and its six-mile-long flume that provided year-round water to the mission. The dam has been restored and is listed on the National Historic Register.

As San Diego's namesake river, it is truly incredible that we have allowed the symbol of the region's natural and cultural history to have been so neglected. Commercial, residential, and industrial development have encroached to the river's edge. Mining operations have excavated the riverbed for sand and gravel. And the lower San Diego River has been listed as an impaired water body because of contamination from polluted urban runoff.

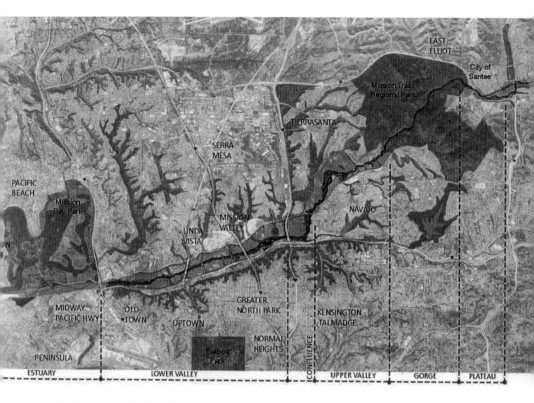

San Diego River Park Master Plan

During my time as mayor, I supported creating a San Diego River Park along the banks of the river from the mountains of the Cleveland National Forest to the Pacific Ocean. To promote that vision, I first organized the San Diego River Alliance, an informal coalition of elected officials from city, county, state, and federal governments interested in developing the river park. To implement the concept, I subsequently teamed up with State Assemblywoman Christine Kehoe to create a new state agency, the San Diego River Conservancy, to fund land acquisition and development of the river park.

Progress to date has been slower than I had hoped. The City of San Diego's San Diego River Park Master Plan, which I called for in my January 2002 State of the City address, is finally nearing completion. Although the San Diego River Foundation has acquired some key parcels, the San Diego River Conservancy's efforts have been somewhat frustrated by limited state government resources. Nevertheless, state park bond funds and Transnet bikeway and environmental mitigation money still provide good opportunities for future funding.

Even though people do not recognize it as such, parts of the San Diego River Park are already in place. The river west of I-5 to the Pacific Ocean runs through Mission Bay Park. Near the eastern boundary of the city of San Diego, the river courses through Mission Gorge in Mission Trails Regional Park. And the First San Diego River Improvement Project (FSDRIP) between Mission Center Road and Qualcomm Way in Mission Valley already incorporates riverside hiking and biking paths.

The next decade provides a unique opportunity to complete much of the San Diego River Park in the city of San Diego. It is just a matter of exploring the available resources. For instance, the Grantville Redevelopment District includes much of the San Diego River from Mission Trails Regional Park to I-15 and could incorporate the river park within its area. Redevelopment of the Riverwalk Golf Club west of Fashion Valley Shopping Center presents another opportunity. And the City-owned land south of Qualcomm Stadium provides yet another chance to expand the river park, especially if the area is redeveloped.

To quote the draft San Diego River Park Master Plan:

The creation of the San Diego River Park is an unprecedented opportunity to take the first steps toward reconnecting the San Diego region with its namesake waterway. Like San Diego's other great parks—Balboa, Mission Trails, and Mission Bay—the San Diego River Park will provide . . . a place of the city rather than a place apart from the city. . . . It will return the river to the people, and integrate the river valley into the life and landscape of San Diego.

PROPOSAL #2:
Develop the San Diego Chargers Office Park

One of the City's challenging tasks is to function as landlord of Qualcomm Stadium. Its prime tenant, the San Diego Chargers, is not satisfied with Qualcomm, and the team has been pushing for years to have a new stadium built. That has presented a difficult political conundrum. Most San Diegans want the Chargers to stay in San Diego, but polls have shown that the majority of San Diegans do not want to spend taxpayer money to build a new football stadium. So the goal is to find a fiscally responsible way to keep the Chargers in town that the public will support.

One proposal under consideration is for a new football stadium to be built downtown. It may be feasible if redevelopment funds are available. But if the local economy and the City continue to hobble along financially, it will be difficult to convince San Diego voters to approve hundreds of millions of tax dollars for a new downtown football stadium.

In my opinion, there is a viable alternative. It would be a modified version of the proposals submitted by the Chargers Task Force that I created and later resurrected by the Citizens for Qualcomm Site Redevelopment. Under this concept, the City would give the San Diego Chargers a long-term lease at a nominal rent on most of the existing 166-acre stadium site in Mission Valley. The Chargers, along with the National Football League and possibly San Diego State University, supplemented with naming rights revenues, could build a new stadium on part of the property. The land between the San Diego Trolley tracks and the San Diego River would become part of the San Diego River Park. The Chargers would be free to develop the balance of the property.

The Chargers, as well as some other civic leaders, floated a similar proposal in the past. But earlier discussions suggested massive residential development on the Qualcomm site. I would argue that the better course would be to allow the Chargers to develop commercial office buildings, creating the San Diego Chargers Office Park. The parking lots or garages used by those working in the office buildings during the week would be used by the Chargers and the SDSU Aztecs on weekends. While hotel or retail uses would be permitted, I would be concerned that residential development would be incompatible with the noise and traffic of a football stadium.

Of course, the City would be handing over more than 100 acres of valuable real estate in Mission Valley. However, the City currently loses money on that property anyway. This proposal would generate property tax, sales tax, and transit occupancy tax revenues for the City.

If redevelopment law survives in some form, the City could explore adding the stadium site to the Grantville Redevelopment District. The Qualcomm site would arguably qualify as a redevelopment zone because soil contamination from the nearby tank farm has caused significant blight. This would allow using the property tax increment to further develop the San Diego River Park east of I-15.

In summary, I believe a new San Diego Chargers football stadium at Qualcomm has three advantages:

1. It keeps the stadium at a familiar central location with access to three freeways and a San Diego Trolley stop.
2. It requires little financial risk for the City and no upfront costs.
3. It augments the San Diego River Park and offers an opportunity for further enhancement upstream.

PROPOSAL #3:
Extend the San Diego Trolley on I-15

I grew up riding fixed rail transit from the western suburbs to downtown Chicago. I loved the safety, reliability, and smooth ride that fixed rail provides. So when I had the opportunity to serve two years as chair of the Metropolitan Transit Development Board (MTDB) in the early 1980s, I worked with MTDB General Manager Tom Larwin and his staff to develop a San Diego Trolley master plan, which would extend light rail transit east to El Cajon, north to UCSD, and through Mission Valley to San Diego State.

San Diego County's rail transit system has come a long way since the 1980s. The San Diego Trolley Blue Line now serves South Bay, the Orange Line serves East County, and the Green Line serves Mission Valley. The Coaster runs north-south from Oceanside to downtown San Diego. The Sprinter, another light-rail system run by the North County Transit District, travels east-west from Oceanside to Escondido. But what is still missing is a north-south inland fixed-rail transit line from Mission Valley north to Escondido. Such a line would complete a light-rail transit framework that, interconnected to feeder bus routes, would serve the entire region.

The planned San Diego Trolley Mid-Coast extension from Old Town to UCSD and University Town Centre is a worthwhile project. But the next project after that should be a San Diego Trolley extension along Interstate 15 from Qualcomm Stadium to the eastern terminus of the Sprinter in Escondido, with stops in Kearny Mesa, MCAS Miramar, Mira Mesa, Rancho Penasquitos, Rancho Bernardo, and Westfield North County Fair. I doubt that the proposed Bus Rapid Transit along I-15 will ever generate enough ridership to significantly reduce traffic congestion.

My background and experience suggests that an inland line along Interstate 15 would be feasible. In addition to serving as chair of MTDB,

I served as the City's representative on the San Diego Association of Governments (SANDAG) Board of Directors and Transportation Committee during my first term as mayor. Working with SANDAG Executive Director Gary Gallegos, I proposed the regional government restructuring that added mass transit planning and development to SANDAG's responsibilities, as well as its unique bicameral-weighted voting system, which protects the interests of both large and small cities.

Based on my experience, I believe that SANDAG's 2050 Regional Transportation Plan should include a San Diego Trolley extension along I-15 between Qualcomm Stadium and Escondido. There are ample revenues from the Transnet half-cent sales tax to fund this project. None of San Diego should be left out of the San Diego Trolley network.

PROPOSAL #4:
Create a New Park to Bay Link

One of the 1908 Nolen Plan proposals was a grand paseo that would link Balboa Park and San Diego Bay, known as the "Park to Bay Link." Nolan's paseo plan, which would have run east and west between Date and Elm streets, was never implemented. However, the time may be right to resurrect the concept on a new route.

Of course, park to bay links already exist, sort of. Laurel Street connects Balboa Park and San Diego Bay. However, the western half of the street would need a dramatic overhaul to be attractive, and there is no obvious funding source. If the California Public Utility Commission ever approves a railroad crossing at Harbor Drive, Park Boulevard will link Balboa Park to the Bay. But the San Diego Trolley tracks down the middle of Park Boulevard between C and K Streets would need to be removed in order to create a truly grand thoroughfare.

My recommendation is to create a new park to bay link that would travel south from Balboa Park on Park Boulevard and turn west on

Broadway to San Diego Bay. Broadway has the physical width to be the ceremonial street that Nolen envisioned. In my opinion, the Centre City Development Corporation has the funds to provide the improvements. And completion of the first phase of the North Embarcadero Visionary Plan, the redevelopment of North Harbor Drive along San Diego Bay west of downtown, will provide an impressive terminal point where Broadway meets the Bay.

Ideally, there will be two mini-parks at the foot of Broadway—at the southeast and northeast corners of North Harbor Drive and Broadway. Each mini-park could include a large, iconic sculpture that would signal the arrival at a dramatic gateway to the city. If the North Embarcadero Visionary Plan is to be San Diego's front porch, the west end of Broadway should be San Diego's front door.

PROPOSAL #5:
Build a New City Hall

When I was elected mayor in 2000, I thought the three highest priority building projects for the City were the downtown ballpark, the main library, and a new city hall—in that order. I hoped to complete the ballpark by 2004, the central library by 2008, and a new city hall by 2012. Unfortunately, the City's pension problems derailed the timetable, but the merits of all three projects remain unchanged.

The present city hall is a civic disgrace. It is an unattractive, outdated, and inefficient 50-year-old derelict in dire need of millions of dollars of electrical, plumbing, and structural repair. It is a health and safety risk to the public and employees alike—contaminated with asbestos, vulnerable to earthquakes, and in violation of fire safety codes. City hall could be a death trap during a fire or an earthquake.

There have been years of discussions and plans aimed at building a new city hall. So far, the result has been proposals and plans—but no action. Perhaps the city council is reluctant to push ahead partly out of fear the public might think the City is merely trying to upgrade its employees' offices. But that is only partly true. City hall is inconvenient for the public as well as for the workers. City council meetings are held on the 12th floor, and people attending these sessions can expect long waits for the old, slow elevators.

As for funding, the City really cannot afford the cost of doing nothing. Although it may seem counterintuitive, a new city hall will actually save taxpayer money. Because of city hall's limited size, the City currently leases hundreds of thousands of square feet to house employees in private office buildings scattered throughout San Diego. Rents will inevitably continue to rise. Expert financial analysis and common sense both indicate that it will be cheaper to own than to rent over the long haul in San Diego. And consolidating City operations in one central location should be more efficient and, therefore, less costly.

A new federal courthouse at Broadway and State Street downtown is under construction. State and County governments are also in the early stages of building a new courthouse at Union and C Streets downtown. With many City leases in private office buildings due to expire in the next few years, now is the time for a new city hall downtown. As a matter of civic pride, San Diegans deserve a city hall they can be proud of

PROPOSAL #6:
Restore Balboa Park's Pan-American Plaza

For years, Balboa Park supporters have been trying to rid the cars from the park's central plazas and reserve that precious space for pedestrians. That is why the fundraising effort led by philanthropist Irwin Jacobs should be roundly applauded. He proposes to restore the Plaza de Panama on Balboa Park's Prado in time for the 100th anniversary of the 1915 Panama-California Exposition. The Jacobs proposal would remove the 67 parking spaces on the Plaza de Panama and return it to a pedestrian-only zone. In addition, the plan would construct a bypass from the east

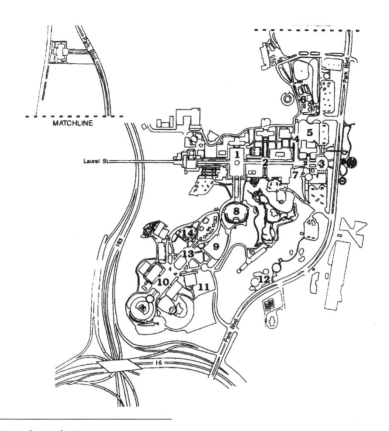

1. Plaza de Panama
2. The Prado
3. Plaza de Balboa
4. Village Promenade
5. Moreton Bay Fig Tree Lawn
6. Spanish Village Plazas
7. Zoro Garden
8. Organ Pavilion
9. Organ Pavilion
   Parking Garage Plaza
10. Plaza de las Americas
11. Lawn Ampitheater
12. Cultural Plaza
13. Palisades Plaza & Lawns
14. House of Pacific Relations Lawn

Balboa Park Central Mesa Precise Plan

end of the Cabrillo Bridge through the Alcazar Garden parking lot to an 800-space parking garage south of the Spreckels Organ Pavilion.

During my time as mayor, we considered implementing the simpler restoration of the Plaza de Panama called for in the Balboa Park Central Mesa Precise Plan. That plan would have removed all parking from the Plaza de Panama and restored most of the plaza as a pedestrian space. However, it simply routed traffic through the southwest corner of the plaza. It did not include the bypass.

In my opinion, it is hard to justify the cost of building a new parking garage on the Organ Pavilion parking lot just to replace the 67 parking spots removed from the Plaza de Panama. It might be justified, however, if it also replaced the parking on the Pan-American Plaza, the huge asphalt parking lot north of the Air and Space Museum. Removing the parking from the Pan-American Plaza and restoring it to its 1935 California Pacific Exposition grandeur has been a long-time dream of Balboa Park lovers. This alternative could be phased: First, Plaza de Panama by 2015, next the Organ Pavilion parking garage and, finally, the Pan-American Plaza restoration. (The Pan-American Plaza is referred to as the Plaza de las Americas in the Balboa Park Central Mesa Precise Plan.)

So how do we pay for the restoration of the Pan-American Plaza in addition to the Plaza de Panama? One solution would be to take funds planned for the bypass and redirect them to restoring the Pan-American Plaza. Another feasible but more controversial solution is for the City to lease the land south of Presidents Way and east of Park Boulevard for development of a boutique hotel, with all lease revenues and transient occupancy taxes from the hotel dedicated to Balboa Park capital improvements and facility maintenance. The precedent has already been set in Mission Bay Park. What would Balboa Park lose? Not much. The hotel would operate on the fringe of Balboa Park, in an area now notable for its parking lots.

PROPOSAL #7:
Expand Lindbergh Field onto MCRD

When I worked with State Senator Steve Peace, City Councilmember Byron Wear, and others to create the San Diego County Regional Airport Authority, I had hoped we could find a new site for Lindbergh Field. My personal choice for a new airport would have been a joint venture with Orange County to build a new Southern California airport somewhere on Camp Pendleton. However, I was not surprised that the new airport authority eventually recommended building a new commercial airport at Marine Corps Air Station Miramar (MCAS Miramar).

During the U.S. Department of Defense Base Realignment and Closure (BRAC) process from 2003 to 2005, I devoted considerable effort as mayor, along with Julie Meyer Wright and the San Diego Economic Development Corporation, to lobby the Navy and Marine Corps not to close any of their bases in San Diego County, including MCAS Miramar. This effort to influence the BRAC decision helped save virtually every military facility in San Diego County from closure. San Diego can boast that it is the largest military complex in the United States. Those facilities are vital to national security as well as the economy of the San Diego region.

So if I had still been mayor when the new Airport Authority recommended relocating Lindbergh Field to MCAS Miramar, it would have been somewhat hypocritical for me to have strongly supported that proposal by urging a Yes vote at the ballot box. That doesn't mean I am opposed to relocating Lindbergh to Miramar. But I would have taken a more nuanced approach in crafting such a ballot measure. I would have suggested alternative ballot language such as: "Should MCAS Miramar remain a military installation as long as it is critical to national defense and be considered for a commercial airport only if the Department of Defense determines it is no longer needed?" My language would have had a better chance of approval by voters and would have left open the Miramar option for the future.

One little-known opportunity that arose during the BRAC process is that the Commandant of the Marine Corps offered to consider turning over the Marine Corps Recruit Depot (MCRD) to expand Lindbergh Field if the City could obtain funding to relocate the MCRD facilities to Camp Pendleton. I declined to pursue it at the time because it would have been inconsistent with the City's BRAC message and the Airport Authority's effort to identify a new airport site. However, now that it appears that Lindbergh Field will not be moving anytime soon, the Airport Authority, at its expense, should attempt to reopen negotiations with the U.S. Marine Corps to expand the airport onto MCRD.

PROPOSAL #8:
Promote Solar Energy Carports

When I was elected mayor in November 2000, California was in the throes of an energy crisis. Electricity shortages triggered rolling blackouts and skyrocketing prices. But the energy crisis also created an opportunity for the City to pursue alternative energy resources. So in 2001, the City of San Diego began a quest to promote solar energy. The initial effort was modest: generate 50 megawatts from solar systems, install solar panels on City buildings, and create a Sustainable Energy Advisory Board to promote solar energy in the private sector. Since then—with a boost from state rebates, federal tax credits, and California Public Utility Commission mandates—the solar movement has gained momentum. Rooftop solar systems have sprouted. Large solar arrays in the desert are being developed.

During the next decade, the City should be focusing its effort at promoting commercial-grade solar projects within the utility grid throughout San Diego. My personal favorite is installing solar panels on top of parking lots adjacent to shopping malls, office buildings, hospitals, schools, and government facilities. The City of San Diego achieved its first energy-independent facility in 2002 by placing solar panels over the parking lot of the City's Environmental Services Building. Not only do solar carports provide large urban areas to collect solar energy, they are not intrusive and protect cars from the sun. The key is that San Diego Gas & Electric (SDG&E) must pay customers if they produce more electricity than they use.

Not only does solar energy improve air quality, reduce greenhouse gas emissions, and reduce our dependence on imported fossil fuels, it provides fixed-cost-dependable energy supplies. Reliable, low-cost energy is critical to the long-term economic growth of the region. As fossil fuel supplies shrink during the 21st century, cities with alternative methods for generating electricity will prosper. With abundant solar resources, San Diego is uniquely positioned to provide a future of energy security.

PROPOSAL #9:
Pursue More Ocean Water Desalination Facilities

Water is San Diego's lifeblood. We live in a desert where rainfall is scarce and unpredictable. Today the San Diego region imports approximately 90 percent of its water from Northern California and the Colorado River. And the San Diego County Water Authority, led by General Manager Maureen Stapleton, has done an outstanding job of securing additional imported water resources.

Nevertheless, the supply of imported water is always threatened by drought, environmental restraints, and political infighting among intra-state and interstate government entities. Rainwater and groundwater can provide only a fraction of the region's needs. Conservation is important, but it too has limits. Recycling wastewater is great for irrigation, but the verdict is still out on potable water reuse. The only certain way to guarantee adequate water supplies for the region in the long run is large-scale ocean water desalination.

The San Diego region has a huge strategic advantage over other cities in the Southwest. It is located on the edge of an unlimited water supply—the Pacific Ocean. All we need to do is tap into it. But the struggle to build San Diego's first large-scale ocean water desalination plant in Carlsbad has taken more than a decade. One of the San Diego County Water Authority's top priorities for the second decade of the 21st century should be to accelerate the construction of more desalination plants in San Diego County.

Like energy, reliable, low-cost water supplies are critical to the long-term economic growth of the region. As population growth and climate change inevitably increase the demand for fresh water, metropolitan areas that can provide reliable water supplies will thrive. With the world's largest reservoir—the Pacific Ocean—at our doorstep, desalination has the potential to make San Diego drought-proof and water self-sufficient.

PROPOSAL #10:
Celebrate San Diego's 250th Birthday with a New Entry into Old Town

On Sunday, July 16, 1769, Spanish Franciscan priest Father Junipero Serra founded the first mission in present-day California by celebrating mass on Presidio Hill in San Diego. That date is celebrated as the day the City of San Diego was founded. The mission, along with a military fort, became the first permanent European settlement in California. The pueblo that developed below Presidio Hill is today Old Town San Diego State Historic Park.

In the year 2019, the City of San Diego will celebrate its 250th birthday. This will be an important historic milestone for both the city and for the state, since modern California also began with the founding of the mission on Presidio Hill. Such a significant milestone deserves a fitting project to honor San Diego right where it was founded.

There is a suitable way for San Diego and California to celebrate its 250th birthday at its birthplace. This could be done by demolishing the former California Department of Transportation (Caltrans) office buildings at the southwest corner of Juan and Taylor Streets, restoring the site to reflect the cultural landscape of 19th century Old Town, and adding it to the neighboring Old Town San Diego State Historic Park. If properly redeveloped to include closure of Wallace and Calhoun Streets, removal of the adjacent parking lot, and demolition of non-historic buildings, the site could provide an impressive entryway to the heart of the park.

Since the site is state-owned, funding for the restoration project should come from the State of California. Caltrans should pay for the demolition of its former headquarters because the old structure is riddled with hazardous materials such as asbestos and lead paint. The State Parks Department should perform the restoration work on the Caltrans site, possibly with the use of State park bond money.

Imagine that grand new entrance into one of San Diego's most popular visitor destinations. Now that would be something San Diegans could celebrate in 2019!

Conclusion

Realization of any of these 10 proposals would help move the city closer to the objective of creating a city worthy of our affection. And while some would require a change in City policies, these ideas are not mere whimsy. To ensure they can be achieved, I have suggested potential ways to finance each project.

Years ago, at the dawn of modern San Diego, Nolen believed that San Diego had the leadership to match its potential. He thought San Diego was destined for greatness. It had everything going for it, especially a near-perfect climate and a beautiful seaside location with rugged cliffs, canyons, and hills. He had confidence in the leadership abilities of San Diego's civic-minded citizens. "Its people are awake to its needs, and are resolved to meet them," Nolen said.

Now, a century later, not all of Nolen's concepts have been accomplished, but I think, in some larger measure, he would find that his faith in San Diego's leaders has been rewarded. Surely, he would be dazzled by the downtown skyline, the Gaslamp Quarter, the downtown ballpark, the promenades along the bay, the sleek red trolleys, Balboa Park and Mission Bay, miles of pristine beaches, as well as San Diego's many distinctive neighborhoods stretching for miles in every direction.

Nolen had one quality that never goes out of style and is absolutely necessary to move the city forward, regardless of the trends, tastes, or controversies of the moment. He was an enthusiastic optimist. He believed—as I do—that San Diego's civic leaders would find the means to continue improving the city long after he left the scene.

It is in that spirit—and with great hope—that I pass the torch to San Diego's future visionaries.

INDEX

ACKNOWLEDGMENTS

Writing and publishing a book involves much more than simply putting pen to paper. It takes a team. I was fortunate to have a great one.

First and foremost, my publishing consultant and editor, Karla Olson of BookStudio, was an indispensible guide through the labyrinth of book publishing.

My two literary collaborators, Dale Fetherling and Lynne Carrier, along with copyeditor Laurie Gibson, applied their outstanding writing skills to sculpt the story I wrote into more readable prose.

My book cover and interior design consultant Lydia D'moch utilized her terrific artistic talents to create an attractive book layout and jacket.

Finally, I appreciate the confidence shown by Lowell and Diana Lindsay of Sunbelt Publications for publishing and distributing this book.

—JUDGE/MAYOR DICK MURPHY
SEPTEMBER 2011

About the Author

DICK MURPHY was born in Oak Park, Illinois and grew up in the west suburbs of Chicago. He was in the first graduating class from Proviso West High School in Hillside, where he was senior class president and captain of the basketball team.

He graduated Phi Beta Kappa with a B.A. in economics from the University of Illinois. Subsequently, he received a Master of Business Administration (M.B.A.) from Harvard University and law degree (J.D.) from Stanford University.

He served as a U.S. Army officer in the Pentagon and the White House, as the San Diego Regional Marketing Director for Bank of America, and as an attorney with the law firm of Luce, Forward, Hamilton & Scripps.

He was an elected member of the San Diego City Council from 1981 to 1985. This period launched the transformation of downtown San Diego with the approval of the Horton Plaza Shopping Center and the San Diego Convention Center.

During this period, he chaired the Metropolitan Transit Development Board. Under his leadership, funding for the East Line of the San Diego Trolley was secured and construction began.

During the same time, he chaired the Mission Trails Regional Park Task Force. Working with other community leaders, he led the effort to create Mission Trails Regional Park, one of the largest urban parks in America.